PRAISE FOR
ELEVATED ECONOMICS

"Through compelling real-world examples, *Elevated Economics* makes a strong case that purpose and stakeholder focus are core elements of successful businesses. Driven by consumers and investors, this trend is only accelerating, and corporate leadership who ignore it do so at their peril."

—VIKRAM GANDHI, senior lecturer, **Harvard Business School**

"Richard Steel has written a playbook for navigating the new business paradigm that we all find ourselves immersed in. Our customers and candidates expect and deserve more. *Elevated Economics* lays out intentional and actionable steps backed by data to help us all best adapt to this fast changing landscape."

—AARON KRALJEV, former vice president, **Wells Fargo**

"As an impact investor, I appreciate Steel's recognition of how essential new attitudes towards investing will be to building a new economy that serves us all. His breadth of experience and concrete examples make *Elevated Economics* an important and actionable guide."

—MORGAN SIMON, founding partner, **Candide Group**

"Richard Steel reminds us that there is more to life and business than maximizing shareholder value. When Harvard Business School was created, Dean Edwin Gay said, 'The purpose of business is to make a decent profit decently.' That's what sensible investors will demand of the management teams they back."

—**WILLIAM SAHLMAN,** professor, **Harvard Business School**

"The old way of doing business is already dead—it just doesn't know it yet. *Elevated Economics* delivers an essential wake-up call to business leaders to embrace the future, illuminating what has changed and how they must adapt. I highly recommend this book to anyone looking to win in this new economy."

—**DREW FRASER,** CEO, **Method Products**

"*Elevated Economics* ties together three powerful discontinuities facing all companies: customers behaving differently, investors acting differently, and competitors responding differently. Steel frames a powerful argument for change with a pragmatic approach on 'how to.'"

—**GEORGE RIEDEL,** senior lecturer, **Harvard Business School**

"*Elevated Economics* is a must-read for every business leader. Consumers are increasingly making purchasing decisions based on a new paradigm. Richard Steel identifies this new reality and offers solutions all in one fell swoop. Leaders will be using this book to rethink their marketing and product strategy for years to come."

—**ROB HOWARD,** vice president, **Target**

"*Elevated Economics* persuasively makes the case, aligned with what we see in the millions of reviews of companies on Glassdoor, that companies with a strong sense of mission and purpose outperform their peers. Doing the right thing and shareholder returns are not in conflict. Companies that do good attract the best talent and connect more deeply with their customers, which is ultimately good for business."

—CHRISTIAN SUTHERLAND-WONG, CEO, Glassdoor

"We are at a turning point in the history of capitalism. Companies are becoming accountable not only for their economic performance but for their contribution to shared value. Richard Steel offers a blueprint for how to leverage and contribute to today's changes by focusing on purpose, inclusion, and social and environmental progress. Business leaders–from aspiring entrepreneurs to managers of the largest enterprises–will benefit from his timely insight."

—SCOTT STERN, professor, MIT

"The world is different now and businesses have to adjust. *Elevated Economics* helps guide decision makers to make smart choices, and when done correctly, both the consumer and company win."

—BLAKE MYCOSKIE, founder, TOMS Shoes

ELEVATED ECONOMICS

HOW CONSCIOUS
CONSUMERS WILL FUEL
THE FUTURE OF BUSINESS

RICHARD STEEL

FAST
COMPANY
Press

Fast Company Press
New York, New York
www.fastcompanypress.com

Distributed by Greenleaf Book Group

For ordering information or special discounts for bulk purchases, please contact Greenleaf Book Group at PO Box 91869, Austin, TX 78709, 512.891.6100.

Design and composition by Greenleaf Book Group
Cover design by Greenleaf Book Group
Image: Abraham Lincoln Golden one dollar coin isolated on white background, used under license from Shutterstock.com

Publisher's Cataloging-in-Publication data is available.

Print ISBN: 978-1-7343248-4-6

eBook ISBN: 978-1-7343248-5-3

Part of the Tree Neutral® program, which offsets the number of trees consumed in the production and printing of this book by taking proactive steps, such as planting trees in direct proportion to the number of trees used: www.treeneutral.com

TreeNeutral®

Printed in the United States of America on acid-free paper

20 21 22 23 24 25   10 9 8 7 6 5 4 3 2 1

First Edition

To my family

CONTENTS

INTRODUCTION

T he only constant is change.

To prepare for change is to prepare for success. If you can get in front of a change, you create an opportunity for yourself, for your business, and for your industry. This book is my attempt to draw attention to a huge change in the economic landscape—a change so massive it's already earned its place on the Mt. Rushmore of disruption, right alongside the Industrial Revolution and the rise of big tech.

My purpose here is to provide a look forward at how the changing behaviors of consumers and investors are irrevocably shaping the business cycle of this decade and the ones to come. These are not small changes, and the consequences of ignoring them won't be small either.

If you are a business leader or someone with any influence over the decisions your company makes, then the information and analysis presented in this book will serve as your guide into a brave new world, a world where consumers have begun to do the one thing that the capitalists of the last 150 years feared: care. Not just about product, price, place, and promotion. But, as Bianca Gates, CEO of Birdies, so eloquently articulated, consumers care about the new "P" of business that is a result of today's informed, connected, and imperiled consumer class: Purpose.[1]

The data used to form this picture of the future comes from both primary and secondary sources. I conducted interviews with CEOs and leaders on the front lines. We talked about what's coming and about what has already arrived. I talked with Ivy League professors of business, marketing, and consumer behavior. Their research combined with the experiences of some of the most exciting young executives working today help form the backbone of this story. I also draw from my own experience running public and private companies, and from countless hours poring over research, dissecting charts and graphs, and extrapolating trend lines. I guess you could call me an obsessed lunatic; but to paraphrase the great Billy Joel, when this much change starts occurring at this speed, I "just might be the lunatic you're looking for."

Whether you call it a forecast, a blueprint, a manual, or a road map, if you are a leader, or someone who aspires to be in a leadership position, this book will be your companion as you lead your company into the future with confidence.

That future is fluid, chaotic, and rapidly iterating. Setting your firm up for success in this sort of environment won't be as simple as adjusting a few sentences on your mission statement. This is a street fight. If you don't keep your hands up and your eyes open, you'll likely find yourself knocked out—trampled by a stampede of radically altered consumers.

But if you do come to fight, and prepare to fight well, then the potential upside is immense. With some motivation, training, and just a few well-placed blows, you may find your firm's fist being raised

---

1 Bianca Gates, in discussion with the author, December 2019.

to the sky in victory. The training is in the following pages. The motivation is here. Taking action is up to you. It won't be an easy journey, but at the end you may emerge victorious: a champion of a brand-new economy. A better economy, an Elevated Economy.

CHAPTER 1

UP AND TO THE RIGHT

"Anyone can hold the helm when the sea is calm."
—Publilius Syrus

E verybody thinks Chernobyl exploded.

They picture flashing lights and blaring alarms as the power plant erupted into a morbidly fantastic mushroom cloud. They picture something immediate and spectacular. They picture a single moment of disaster. But that's not how it happened.

On February 21, 1979, Yuri Andropov—then chairman of the KGB—filed a report. Two years before, construction on the now-infamous nuclear power plant had been completed, deep behind Ukraine's Iron Curtain. As a dutiful servant of his beloved Soviet Union, Andropov felt compelled to alert his superiors to some errors he had been made aware of in the plant's construction. If ignored, Andropov wrote, these flaws might "lead to failures and accidents."

The report was sent, delivered, and completely ignored. Chernobyl was the crown jewel in the Soviet's nuclear kingdom. In their rapidly expanding effort to compete with the West's nuclear power plants, weapons, and technology, it was easier to ignore Andropov's report than it would have been to admit defeat, flaws, or both.

However, seven years after Andropov's first report, those same superiors received another report. And this one was a lot harder to ignore. Its title was as devastating as its contents: "Urgent Report: Accident at the Chernobyl Atomic Power Station."

There it was. Andropov had been correct. The damage was being done. All the indicators in the plant were showing levels well past the red line. Disaster was imminent. The best action at that point would have been for the government to immediately evacuate the area, repair the breaches, and help the affected citizenry recover.

Except they didn't.

For a report detailing a nuclear meltdown, the most chilling line comes in a moment of shocking bureaucratic detachment: "It is not required to take special measures, including the evacuation of the population from the city."

The Chernobyl disaster occurred on April 26, 1986. Before the close of 1986, two more reports had been filed. These explained that atmospheric and agriculture tests were detecting levels of radiation "dangerous to the health of the population."

By the end of the year, the radiation levels were more than 50 times higher than Soviet standards of safe levels for human exposure. The experts writing these reports projected that at least 4,000 lives would be lost due to radiation poisoning and environmental collapse. But to this day, the true consequences of this disaster remain a closely guarded state secret.

The husk of the power plant that remains, and the surrounding areas, are waiting to become habitable once more. They should be ready in just under 20,000 years.

Delayed reactions, willful ignorance, and pride cost the lives of thousands and made the area around Chernobyl uninhabitable for the next 650 generations.

Everybody thinks Chernobyl exploded without warning. But it didn't.

It leaked.

And that's the real horror. Because while an explosion happens suddenly and without warning, a leak can be patched over. An accidental explosion can take lives and destroy communities. It is sudden, tragic, and unexpected. But a leak has to be tolerated. It has to be recognized. It has to be ignored long enough for it to become a disaster.

The lesson of Chernobyl has little to do with humanity's technological hubris or fate's spite and everything to do with the consequences of intentional inaction. It's a lesson worth revisiting.

Today, the global economy is having its Yuri Andropov moment. The indicator lights aren't yet flashing. The alarms aren't yet blaring, but we are approaching a red line of our own.

CERTIFIED SUSTAINABLE

A friend of mine was having lunch one afternoon at a large outdoor shopping center. The center was under renovation, and many of its new storefronts had yet to be filled. One such lot was emblazoned with a wraparound banner the size of a Buick advertising a new sushi restaurant. Nothing strange about that, but the copy of this particular ad caught his eye:

"The world's first certified-
sustainable sushi restaurant"

And that was it. Nothing about the way the food would taste or how affordable the meals would be. The sole message that this new business wanted passersby to know was not "We're delicious!" or "We're so fresh." Rather, it was "We are sustainable."

As he recounted this to me, I was struck by the laser focus of it all. Because it meant that somewhere, sometime, at some meeting this group of entrepreneurs had decided to build a food business on the back of sustainability. Not price. Not convenience. Not taste. Sustainability. And they aren't alone.

Business has started to change. It's far from omnipresent, but the shift has started.

Tech giants like Facebook and Alphabet are tripping over themselves to show the world how seriously they are taking things like emissions, ethical supply chains, diversity, and employee satisfaction. Fast-food companies are replacing meat with plant-based alternatives. Even Gillette is attacking its core market with advertisements addressing toxic masculinity.

I started my first company in 2000. This wasn't how the world worked back then. Back then the name of the game was convenience; people wanted things easier, cheaper, and faster, and businesses were all too happy to oblige. Door-to-door delivery, digital payments, and online commerce were emerging trends of the early 2000s. A sushi restaurant emblazoned with certified sustainability accolades in 2000 would have been a non sequitur at best, and alienating at worst. One would be right to ask: What happened over the last 20 years?

But the better question is: What is happening now, and what will happen next?

Businesses have always, and will always, act primarily in their own interest. In the same manner, consumers have always, and will always, make purchases that reflect and support their own interests. Commerce lives at the intersection between the self-interests of these two groups, but it's the consumer that really sets the rules of the relationship.

Al Gore can make all the movies he wants. Rising sea levels could have submerged the Eastern seaboard and companies still wouldn't launch environmentally friendly ad campaigns unless they had data showing that consumers actually care enough to buy environmentally friendly products. But when they do care, the opportunity is massive.

Drew Fraser, president and CEO of Method Products, attributes a healthy amount of his company's meteoric success to its environmentally friendly reputation. According to Fraser:

> We want to make sure that these are hardworking heavy-duty cleaning products that also work in ways that are totally sustainable. So it's not just efficacy, the manner in which the product is made and manufactured needs to be sustainable as well. And then style, we want to be a little lighter, a little more whimsical in a very serious category where there's not a lot of fun going on. So, bringing a little color, joy, shape, and design to our products was the way in which we combined fun and function with positive global impact.
>
> . . . These are still small market shares in massive categories. So, there's just tons of upside for these products and brands to continue to scale.[1]

The signs we're seeing now—whether they're splashed across the front page of *The Wall Street Journal* or covering the windows of an upcoming sushi restaurant—are not reflections of a change in

---

1 Drew Fraser, president and CEO of Method Products, in discussion with the author, December 2019.

corporate ethics. They are evidence of a change in consumer behavior. And it's a big change. The signals are all around us.

We are getting closer to another red line: consumer disaffection.

SIGNAL ONE: THE ESG RENAISSANCE

Fortunately for all of us, the state of business is not something that requires guesswork. There are systems, reports, statistics, and tools at our disposal ready to help us diagnose, strategize, and act. When it comes to understanding economic forces, there's still no place like Wall Street.

Over the last few years, and in the last year especially, a certain slice of the market has received a notable amount of increased attention and enhanced relevance: ESG Investing. ESG stands for environmental, social, and governance. Together, E, S, and G comprise the investing world's best attempt to measure the impact of business practices that relate to the good of the planet, society at large, and how firms behave. As Harvard professor Vikram S. Gandhi explained recently: "Impact investments are investments with the intention to generate positive, measurable social and environmental impact alongside a financial return."[2]

More specifically, when we're talking about ESG we are talking about outcomes, specifically externalities. Currently, firms force negative externalities like polluted air or water, poor working conditions, and the like on society at large if those actions result in greater profit maximization. This is the classic behavior illustrated by "the tragedy of the commons"—a situation in a shared-resource system where individual users, acting independently according to their own self-interest, behave contrary to the common good of all users by depleting or spoiling that resource through their collective action.

---

2 Vikram S. Gandhi, lecture at Harvard Business School reunion, September 2019.

But now, investors have more options. They can easily invest in companies or funds that have a positive impact on all users by buying ESG funds, or by directing their money managers to invest in ESG financial products. Only recently have the largest brokerage firms like Vanguard, Schwab, and Fidelity begun to offer ESG mutual funds and ETFs, finally making socially responsible investing—SRI—easy.

In the past it was thought that the investor would have to forego financial returns in exchange for investing in firms that had sound ESG practices, but now it is known that that is not necessarily the case. Firms operating with a focus on sound ESG principles operate with the intent of providing enhanced value to all stakeholders, not just financial shareholders.

Environmental, social, and corporate governance practices are not akin to a firm doing charity work. It is always a twofold effort: to create good and to increase wealth. The two cannot be separated in a proper definition of socially responsible investing. According to Charles Schwab, "For years, critics argued that SRI investors sacrificed performance on the altar of good intentions. While that may have been the case in the past, today's SRI funds have been keeping pace with their non-SRI peers."

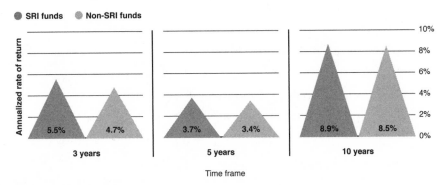

Source: Charles Schwab Investment Advisory, Inc., with data from Morningstar, as of 12/31/2018. Returns represent the average annualized performance of US equity open-end socially responsible and non-socially responsible mutual funds. **Past performance is no guarantee of future returns.** Morningstar defines funds as socially responsible if they invest according to noneconomic guidelines such as environmental responsibility, human rights, or religious views.

My position is that ESG will remain a key trend in the next decade and beyond. Morgan Stanley concurs; in a white paper analyzing risk and returns of sustainable funds, they state that "research conducted on the performance of nearly 11,000 mutual funds . . . shows that there is no financial trade-off in the returns of sustainable funds compared to traditional funds, and they demonstrate lower downside risk."[3] Having sound environmental, social, and corporate governance practices is not a new concept. It predates many other economic trends that have come and gone. However, the ethical investing space is currently experiencing something of a renaissance as society progresses. Simply put: Socially responsible investing and ESG are no longer the hobby of a handful of do-good investors and morally minded brokerage firms. It has become one of the most talked-about sectors of the market. Why? Because for the first time in the history of capitalism, corporations are enacting strategy after strategy from the ESG playbook. And when businesses change, the market—and its investors—notice.

As Robert Eccles, one of the most important ESG economists, said in a recent interview:

> I think we're at the tipping point. I think it's a top priority. I think the degree to which the commitment to "sustainability" or sustainable investing is, it varies. There's data that shows over 50 percent of assets are invested in sustainable investing in Europe. It's about a third in Canada. It's about 25 percent in the United States, which people find surprising. Bank of America Merrill Lynch did a study. They asked their corporate clients what percentage of their assets they thought were held by sustainable investing shops, and they thought it was 5 percent.

---

3 Morgan Stanley, "Sustainable Reality: Analyzing Risk and Returns of Sustainable Funds," August 7, 2019, https://www.morganstanley.com/pub/content/dam/msdotcom/ideas/sustainable-investing-offers-financial-performance-lowered-risk/Sustainable_Reality_Analyzing_Risk_and_Returns_of_Sustainable_Funds.pdf.

So, what you see is, at the top of the house, the chief executive officers, the chief investment officers of the BlackRocks, of the State Streets, or the Vanguards, they know that it's important to take these factors into account from a fiduciary point of view. From a returns point of view.[4]

The numbers back up Eccles's enthusiasm. The following graph from the World Resources Institute demonstrates a rapid rise in the number of investment funds incorporating ESG criteria over a 20-year period. During that time, the total number of funds multiplied over 50 times.

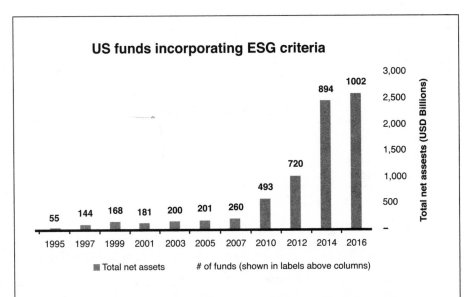

Source: World Resources Institute, US SIF Foundation; The data includes funds that incorporate various ESG criteria and is restricted to mutual funds, variable annuity funds, alternative investments funds, exchange-traded funds, closed-end funds, and other pooled products. It excludes community investing institutions and assets not associated with a dedicated fund or manager. Separate accounts were beginning in 2014 to maintain exclusive focus on commingled products.

4 https://hbr.org/podcast/2019/05/why-its-time-to-finally-worry-about-esg.

A second graph from The Forum for Sustainable and Responsible Investment[5] shows just how potent the rise in total ESG investment activity has been in the United States over the past decade.

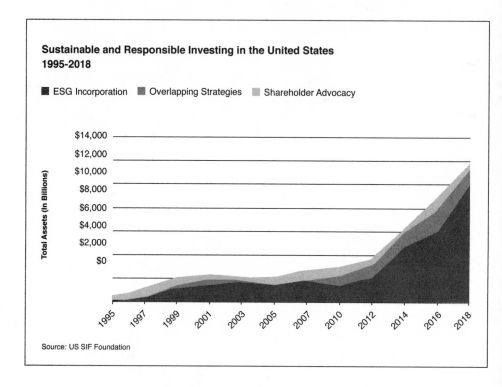

Sustainable and Responsible Investing in the United States 1995-2018

■ ESG Incorporation   ■ Overlapping Strategies   ■ Shareholder Advocacy

Source: US SIF Foundation

Both graphs indicate increasing optimism. The figures are up and to the right all around. Corporate and investor actions that line up with the Socially Responsible Investing/Environmental, Social, and Governance definition are doing better than they ever have. And they show no sign of slowing down. In their April 2020 Global Outlook report, BlackRock forecasts a "tectonic shift to sustainable investing."[6]

---

5 For more on US SIF, see www.ussif.org.

6 BlackRock Global Outlook Report, April 2020, https://www.blackrock.com/corporate/literature/whitepaper/bii-global-outlook-in-charts.pdf.

Today, the total valuation of ESG assets is around $30 trillion. That's more than 25 percent of the managed assets in the entire market. And a generational change will likely take this number even higher. In the next two decades, $40 trillion of wealth will transfer from Baby Boomers to Gen X and Millennials. According to Professor Gandhi, only 22 percent of Boomers express interest in impact investing. For Gen X, it's 31 percent. And Millennials report a massive 71 percent interest in investing in impact-minded corporations willing to toe the ESG line. Gen Z is reported to take this percentage even higher.

It's important to understand the definition of ESG as a two-pronged spear—focusing on creating impact and wealth simultaneously—and the massive uptick in interest for this space. An uptick that is quickly moving from observation, to trend, to best practice.

The message to decision makers is clear: the times are changing. In fact, they've already changed. The tide has turned and the waves are crashing toward the shore. But the companies poised to win aren't the ones running for cover.

They're the ones reaching for their surfboards.

SIGNAL TWO: THE AMAZON EFFECT

For over a decade, tech giants were the best place on earth for a young person to work. The high salaries, interesting challenges, and ample free food of the Facebooks and Googles of the world were enough to entice the best and brightest from across the globe to Silicon Valley.

Today, the influence of tech has spread out of Silicon Valley and around the world. Denver, Columbus, Austin, Tel Aviv, Brisbane, Munich—the tech giants have offices everywhere, and where the giants step, shock waves follow. The FAANGs (Facebook, Apple, Amazon,

Netflix, and Google) have influenced everything—from perks and salaries, to the way an office should be laid out, to work-from-home policies, to the possibility of upward mobility for all workers.

Their influence on the business world has been palpable, and so it was striking when everything hit the fan in 2019. That was the year when thousands of employees rebelled against their tech utopias in protest. Walkouts, refusals to work on unpopular projects, internal leaks, and calls for change were the news du jour. Employee activism was on the rise. But why?

G stands for more than Google. In ESG it stands for governance, which includes the board's standards for company leadership, ethical business practices, board independence and diversity, voting rights, executive pay vs. employee pay, financial and tax transparency, and so on. Governance pertains to the way businesses do business. The same altruistic wind that is driving new consumer behavior and corporate decision-making is driving employees to demand change from the inside, change from the board level all the way to the front lines.

Laela Sturdy, General Partner, CapitalG (formerly Google Capital), demonstrates that the Elevated Economy is thriving. And according to Laela, it starts with a capital G—Governance:

> At CapitalG, we invest in private technology companies at the growth stage. In considering the companies and entrepreneurs that we'll back, we take our responsibility very seriously. We set both a personal bar, and, as a derivative of Google's brand, we adhere to their bar as well.
>
> One of the biggest changes I've seen in institutional investor behavior is the conversation around gender equity. This change, originally propelled by the #MeToo movement, helped people have a conversation around the money value-chain. For

example, people started to [put] pressure on an LP (Limited Partner): We are going to hold you responsible for the diversity and makeup of the GPs (General Partners) that you're backing. And as a GP, we are going to hold you responsible for the diversity of the type of founders you're backing.

It's really an examination of how capital flows through the venture ecosystem and how the decision makers can influence who has access to capital. I am inspired by the examination and pressure that was put on the ecosystem around gender and racial diversity in Venture, but I haven't seen the same positive momentum on the decision-making process in Venture as it relates to social and environment issues.

Climate change is the issue of our age, and it's incredibly important that we all take action. Businesses are going to be central to the leadership of taking appropriate action. And if investors (the source of capital) can help make that change happen faster, that is a good thing for all of us.

The biggest movement I've seen in Venture is around diversity—investors and entrepreneurs considering the capital that they raise and considering if it comes from funds with racial and gender diversity. To me that looks like a good model for other causes as well—both social and environmental.

I have a lot of admiration for everyone in the ecosystem who takes a principled stand around these issues. It means a lot for them to stand up for things that matter.[7]

Even Amazon, which remains one of the most trusted brands in the United States, was cowed by a recent employee walkout. Amazon

---

7   Laela Sturdy, General Partner, CapitalG, in discussion with the author, January 2020.

Employees for Climate Justice were dissatisfied with the way their leadership was handling the climate change crisis. Or, rather, not handling.

The result of the walkout was an almost immediate statement from Amazon founder and CEO Jeff Bezos, followed quickly by a new climate pledge from the company. As part of the pledge, Bezos claims that Amazon will be using 100 percent renewable energy by 2030 and will become completely carbon neutral by 2040. The speed at which companies have been willing and able to resolve the issues brought to light by employees is staggering.

Just recently, I read this in an article: "A global group of 415 investors managing $32 trillion in assets just released a combined statement urging governments to accelerate their actions to mitigate climate change."[8]

This is a far cry from the behavior of the brutal capitalists of the early 1900s who were barely bothered by the deaths of their workers, let alone by their laborers' working conditions.

After meeting her at the Fortune Brainstorm Tech Conference, I had the opportunity to interview Kris Miller, former SVP and chief strategy officer at eBay, to get her take on these rapid iterations. According to Miller:

> eBay is very much a purpose-driven company. It was founded by Pierre Omidyar on the basis that people are basically good, and he founded the company in order to be able to help empower people and create economic opportunity. He founded the company based on people selling to other people with minimal intervention of the platform in between them.

---

8 https://www.forbes.com/sites/trevornace/2018/12/11/with-32-trillion-in-assets-investors-demand-immediate-action-on-climate-change/#75cfc9692b48.

Over time, we have continued to thrive and create additional value on the platform. In the past few years, we have been making pretty significant investments to help bring the legacy platform of eBay into modern technology. We're using AI to make it easier to find the things consumers are looking for—whether that's through image recognition, taking a picture of an item, searching for it on eBay, or being able to bookmark your favorite sellers.

We represent millions of small and medium-sized entrepreneurial sellers around the world. Not just obviously in the US, we have sellers around the world. When we think about what we're doing, we are bringing technology to bear on the core eBay platform to be able to try and bring more value to consumers and to do it in a way that improves the buyer experience and really drives strong economic value for our sellers.[9]

Rhetoric like this is typical of many modern CEOs and corporate executives. The terminology is changing and changing fast. Today, leaders are not only betting big on the value they can create for customers and shareholders, they are also betting big on values.

SIGNAL THREE: THE VOTING MACHINE

"We have to change capitalism."

Those strong words come from Larry Fink, the CEO of BlackRock, in his annual open letter to the world's most powerful CEOs and business leaders.

---

9 Kris Miller, former SVP and chief strategy officer at eBay, in discussion with the author, July 2019.

BlackRock is arguably the most ruthless and relentlessly efficient capitalist engine of the last hundred years. It is the largest financial firm in the world, currently managing nearly $7 trillion in assets—more than the GDPs of Russia, Canada, and the United Kingdom combined.

BlackRock is a juggernaut. And it's Fink's job to make sure it stays that way. Why, then, would he suddenly demand a Wall Street revolution against the very principles that sustain not just his business, but the entire economy?

The answer is simple: Fink's loyalty is not to any one economic principle. He sides with the money. And the money is starting to move.

The postwar economic playbooks don't work anymore. The age of cheap, big, and convenient is coming to an end. The race to the bottom has reached its natural conclusion. The "four P's" that every overeager future MBA learns in the first week of business school have expanded.

Consumers no longer make buying decisions based solely on product, price, place, and promotion. They now make purchases that reflect their own personal values. As we enter a new decade, consumers aren't using their dollars to buy. They are using them to vote. Bianca Gates, CEO of Birdies, says that consumers care about this new fifth P: Purpose, "just as much as they care about the first four P's, sometimes even more."[10]

In the next decade, firms won't be able to win simply by offering the most convenient, cheapest, or cleverly marketed products. They will win by establishing, fostering, and communicating an identity that consumers are willing to vote for. So, what are people willing to vote for? According to a recent Nielsen report:

---

10 Gates, discussion with author.

Nearly half (48%) of US consumers say they would definitely or probably change their consumption habits to reduce their impact on the environment. And these consumers are putting their dollars where their values are, spending $128.5 billion on sustainable fast-moving consumer goods (FMCG) products this year. Since 2014, these influential shoppers have grown sustainable product sales by nearly 20%, with a compound average growth rate (CAGR) that's four times larger than conventional products (3.5% vs. −1.0% comparatively). By 2021, we expect these sustainably minded shoppers to spend up to $150 billion on sustainable FMCG goods, an increase of $14 billion–$22 billion.[11]

Consumers are changing their buying habits by changing the reasons why they buy in the first place. More and more people want to make an impact with every single purchase they make. And, once again, businesses are all too happy to accommodate their desires, and collect their dollars.

Larry Fink throws down this gauntlet fully by concluding:

> To prosper over time, every company must not only deliver financial performance, but also show how it makes a positive contribution to society.
>
> Companies must benefit all of their stakeholders, including shareholders, employees, customers, and the communities in which they operate. Without a sense of purpose, no company, either public or private, can achieve its full potential. It will ultimately lose the license to operate from key stakeholders.

---

11 https://www.nielsen.com/us/en/insights/article/2018/was-2018-the-year-of-the-influential-sustainable-consumer/.

It will succumb to short-term pressures to distribute earnings, and, in the process, sacrifice investments in employee development, innovation, and capital expenditures that are necessary for long-term growth.[12]

Fink is describing a brand-new market driven by a brand-new type of consumer. A consumer driven by values, not value. Consumers who want their purchases to reflect not just their needs and wants, but their hopes, dreams, and aspirations for a better future as well.

In a January 2020 article for *Bloomberg News*, Edna Curran writes:

At a recent World Economic Forum meeting in Davos the discussion turned to the question of "peaks," specifically, whether or not we are witnessing peaks in key drivers of the world economy. Among the topics are climate change, the rise of the new generation and inequality.

Strategists at Bank of America Corp. are already telling clients to brace for a "ground-breaking 'peak decade'" that will disrupt business and investing. Ian Bremmer, a delegate at the World Economy Forum's annual meeting and founder of Eurasia Group, describes this year as a "tipping point."

The theme is captured throughout the Davos program, which contains multiple panels on "stakeholder capitalism" and tackling inequality. Participants will also discuss the future of globalization and whether central banks are out of ammunition.[13]

---

12 https://www.nytimes.com/interactive/2018/01/16/business/dealbook/document-BlackRock-s-Laurence-Fink-Urges-C-E-O-s-to-Focus.html?dlbk.

13 https://www.bloomberg.com/news/articles/2020-01-19/welcome-to-peak-decade-from-globalization-to-central-banks.

Clearly the topics addressed at the World Economic Forum meeting in Davos closely resemble those that consumers and investors are beginning to use when evaluating potential purchases or investments.

As Curran continues, "Here are the hot talking points at Davos":

PEAK GLOBALIZATION?

The era of people, goods, and money flowing increasingly unchecked around the world may have passed its high point as governments pursue protectionism and erect more obstacles to migration. Already there are around 77 physical barriers delineating international borders, compared with 15 in 1989 after the fall of the Berlin Wall, according to Bank of America.

Still, the continued development of the digital economy, rising tourism, and mounting reliance of companies on revenues generated outside their home markets provide room for confidence that globalization is evolving rather than ending.

PEAK CAPITALISM?

JPMorgan Chase & Co. CEO Jamie Dimon and BlackRock founder Larry Fink are among those who have entered the debate over whether companies should better weigh stakeholders such as customers and employees, a departure from the decades-old shareholder-first mindset.

Behind the shift: the rise of populism, concern that wages aren't keeping up with assets such as equities, and fears over climate change.

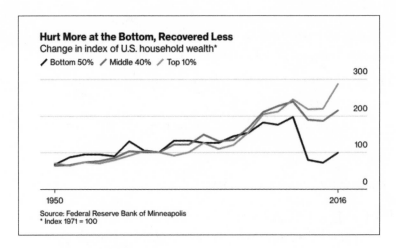

Source: Federal Reserve Bank of Minneapolis

The maturing Millennial generation is a driving force too. When making investment decisions, 87 percent of those born between 1981 and 1996 believe environmental, social, and governance factors are important, according to Bank of America.

PEAK INEQUALITY?

The pressure to reduce inequality will become more urgent this decade as the UN's Sustainable Development Goals approach their 2030 deadline. A total of 193 governments have signed up for 17 goals, 169 targets, and 304 indicators on how to end poverty, clean up the environment, and share prosperity for all.

There has already been some progress. Abhijit Banerjee and Esther Duflo, winners of the 2019 Nobel Prize for economics, estimate that the average income of the world's bottom 50 percent of earners also almost doubled since 1980.

Global Poor

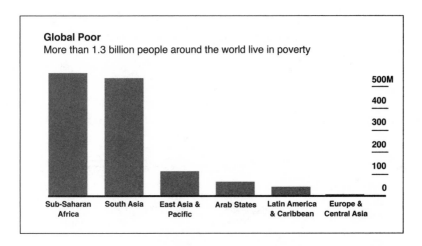

Source: Human Development Report Office 2018

But William Gale of the Brookings Institution notes that the 400 richest Americans owned 3.26 percent of wealth in 2018, up from 0.93 percent in 1982. The top 1 percent also paid about a third of their income in tax in both 1979 and 2019, he says.

PEAK YOUTH?

For the first time, there are now more seniors than children in the world, and that trend is set to escalate, according to the UN.

The global fertility rate already halved from five children per woman in 1955, and the average life expectancy has increased from 31 in 1900 to 72 today and is tipped to reach 83 by the end of this century.

Growing Older

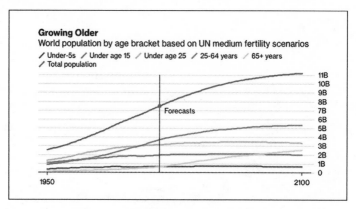

Source: UN Population Division (2017 revision) via Our World in Data

While another billion people are expected on the planet by 2030, the demographic mix will be starkly different. For starters, the number of those aged 65 or older will outnumber children under the age of five.

The growth of the working-age population is also set to slow, straining pensions and healthcare resources. In a recent paper, Stanford University professor Charles Jones said there is a "distinct possibility" that global population will decline rather than stabilize in the long run, threatening economic growth.

PEAK CLIMATE CHANGE?

The world faces a sweeping series of climate-related tipping points— from melting ice caps to droughts and dying coral reefs. *Nature* magazine collated the risks, which they described as a climate emergency that will compel political and economic actions on emissions. Twenty-one of the hottest years on record came in the last quarter century.

"We argue that the intervention time left to prevent tipping could already have shrunk towards zero, whereas the reaction time to achieve net zero emissions is 30 years at best," the article's authors wrote.[14]

The international effort to rein in fossil fuel pollution took a knock in December after marathon UN talks watered down language on issues they had agreed on in previous years.

PEAK OIL DEMAND?

Hotter temperatures have put new scrutiny on the world's energy mix.

Demand Plateau

As seen in the graph below, IEA anticipates a marked slowdown in oil consumption growth.

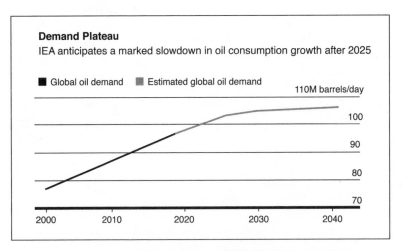

Source: International Energy Agency's 2019 World Energy Outlook

---

14 www.nature.com/articles/d41586-019-03595-0.

This means renewable energy like solar and wind, plus electric vehicles, are going to soar up the policy agenda at the cost of fossil-fuel-gurgling vehicles. Big Oil executives believe that peak oil demand is increasingly likely in the late 2030s.

For example, Saudi Aramco, the world's largest oil producer and the most profitable company on the planet, said on its initial public offering prospectus that oil demand may peak around 2035, with demand "leveling off."

PEAK CARS?

The 1.3 billion vehicles on the roads today are probably the most there will ever be. Megacities will house around two-thirds of the global population by mid-century, cutting back on the need for expensive cars.

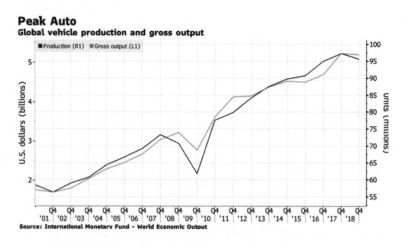

Peak Auto
Global vehicle production and gross output

Source: International Monetary Fund—World Economic Output

Evolving urban architecture will also increasingly constrain car usage. The shift is already underway in mature markets. Only 26 percent of US 16-year-olds earned a driver's license in 2017, compared with almost half just 36 years ago, according to Sivak Applied Research. Even if overall car sales remain robust, cheaper technology such as robotaxis and developments such as ride-sharing stand to take the shine off their attractiveness.

This new consumer is building a new economy altogether: An economy fueled by a desire to improve rather than produce. An economy powered by a society that is determined to pursue not just value, but values. An economy that reflects the aspirations of the people who are now beginning to create it.

An Elevated Economy.

CHAPTER 2

SURVIVAL OF THE PHYSICS

"A kite flies against the wind, not with it."
—**Winston Churchill**

W hat does it mean for the economy to be "Elevated"?

In its simplest terms, the Elevated Economy is my term for a coalescence of several complex factors. Changes in consumer, employment, social, marketing, environmental, and corporate governance practices all contribute to this single term. Essentially, the Elevated Economy represents what research and analysis seem to indicate will be the next great change in capitalism.

In the next few decades, money will move at an unprecedented scale. As the Baby Boomer generation continues to age, retire, and pass away, they are transferring their wealth to Generation X and Millennials. The significance of this cannot be overstated. Because, in addition to being the self-proclaimed "greatest" generation, Baby Boomers also happen to be the richest single generation in history. It is that wealth, above all else, that has allowed them to be the dominant political and socio-economic force in the world. But that's about to change.

Experts are calling this the "Great Wealth Migration."

Roughly 45 million US households will hand down about $68.4 trillion over the course of the next 25 years, according to consulting firm Cerulli Associates.[1]

The Great Wealth Migration will significantly change the answer to the question: Who has the money? The answer to this has typically been a, if not the, key determining factor underlying all business strategies. This won't just be a transfer of wealth; it will be the largest transition of power to ever take place.

According to Cerulli Associates, Baby Boomers currently control about 70 percent of the world's wealth. Over the next decade, all of those assets will begin to move. And move fast. By 2050, Millennials won't just be the richest generation on the planet, they will become the new richest group of humans the world has ever seen. All of that money has to go somewhere, and any corporation worth its salt is preparing to pivot itself to be in line with the consideration set of its next customers and investors. These are customers and investors with different worldviews than the last generation. The issue, however, is that most business leaders are underestimating just how big that pivot needs to be.

This huge shift in assets will likely have profound effects on investment practices and purchase decisions, as Millennials hold much different priorities that will inform how they decide to invest.

The Millennial generation is significantly smaller in population than the Baby Boomers. This means that once the Great Wealth Migration happens, fewer people will be in charge of larger amounts of wealth. Business leaders will have an entirely new "Economic Man"

1　http://info.cerulli.com/rs/960-BBE-213/images/HNW-2018-Pre-Release-Factsheet.pdf.

to contend with. But this Economic Man has evolved and progressed more quickly and in different ways than most were initially predicting. The key to business success in the next quarter century will boil down to how well your business is able to understand and connect with the new decision makers.

Doing so can be complicated and subjective; but, in essence, the mission is the same for everyone. The most significant change wrought by the Elevated Economy is that it has introduced a new fundamental pillar of business into the equation. As discussed in chapter 1, the "four P's" have now become five. Product, price, place, and promotion just got a little brother—purpose—which is quickly beginning to dominate its siblings.

In the Elevated Economy, purpose is just as inexorably linked to the potential success of a business as the P's that came before it. In fact, for the next 30 years or so, purpose will be the single most important pillar for any business to be building. It has become this important because of its significance to one group: Millennials.

The new "richest generation" is going to have more money, more power, and more information than their predecessors. Corporate success in the next three decades and beyond will be almost exclusively decided by this group. They will have more dollars to vote with, and much more specific criteria for those votes, than generations past.

There is nothing "typical" about what's currently happening in the global economy. This is not a gentle curve on the road of capitalism. It is a 180-degree hairpin, tire-skidding reversal. And, even though it is still in its nascent stages, major corporate engines are already shifting gears in order to make the turn. Because while there may be prosperity beyond the hairpin, shrewd business leaders are recognizing that, for right now, the immediate concern is to avoid crashing into the wall.

THE WALL

The reason that "purpose" has been forged into the pantheon of foundational business principles—and the reason why it is becoming the most important of all five—is that customers are beginning to do something they have never done before: care.

Recently, Deloitte completed a yearlong effort to try to understand who the consumers of tomorrow really are. In their own words:

> We scoured government data; talked to clients, industry leaders, and analysts; conducted primary interviews; and surveyed a representative sample of more than 4,000 consumers from the United States. Working with Deloitte's Center for Consumer Insights, we conducted primary research, leveraging 450 billion unique points of location data and more than 200 billion points of credit card transactions. Our goal was to examine the current state of the consumer as well as to study their behavior and underlying attributes to see if there were nuances and intricacies that were being missed.[2]

The results of this study represent a gold mine full of some of the most comprehensive and overlooked insights into the people who are already deciding the future of the global economy. This study provides a rough sketch of these new, elevated consumers and can give business leaders their best look yet at what's changing and how they can and should be following suit. And it all begins with diversity.

According to the study:

---

2 https://www2.deloitte.com/us/en/insights/industry/retail-distribution/the-consumer-is-changing.html.

There is a seismic shift that has taken place in the United States over the past 50 years. The population has become increasingly heterogeneous: Millennials, now representing 30 percent of the population, are the most diverse generational cohort in US history, with roughly 44 percent consisting of ethnic and racial minorities. In comparison, only 25 percent of baby boomers belong to ethnic and racial minorities.

. . . This shows that we have moved to a diverse, splintered, and heterogeneous consumer base with a much broader and varied set of demands and needs. Moreover, the upcoming Gen Z cohort is likely to bring further diversification of the consumer base along racial and ethnic lines.[3]

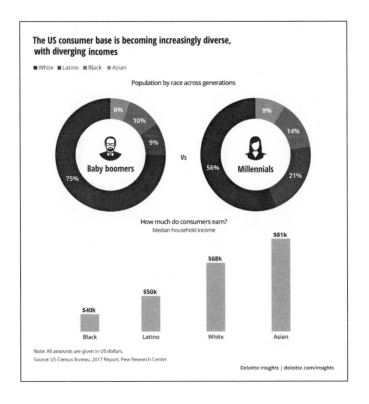

The US consumer base is becoming increasingly diverse, with diverging incomes

■ White ■ Latino ■ Black ■ Asian

Population by race across generations

Baby boomers: 6%, 10%, 9%, 75%

Vs

Millennials: 9%, 14%, 21%, 56%

How much do consumers earn?
Median household income

Black $40k
Latino $50k
White $68k
Asian $81k

Note: All amounts are given in US dollars.
Source: US Census Bureau, 2017 Report, Pew Research Center.

Deloitte Insights | deloitte.com/insights

3 Ibid.

The dominoes are falling, and falling fast. This level of demographic evolution is unprecedented in business history. The markets you can sell to, and the best ways to reach those markets, used to be defined by a single playbook. Now, business leaders will need multiple playbooks, each just as intentional as the one that came before. However, the original playbook was perfected over decades, whereas these new strategies need to be started from scratch. And we're already running behind.

Harvard Business School professor emeritus Bill Sahlman sees those dominoes as global. There's a significant network effect to the Elevated Economy. Purpose-driven businesses are doing what traditional businesses have done for generations: benefit from the effort and innovation of one another. According to Sahlman, one good example of this is solar energy as a renewable resource.

"Solar exists today as a viable option because the Chinese invested $25 billion in manufacturing and research," Sahlman told me. "The Germans spent billions and billions of dollars subsidizing, which is the same as putting a tax on carbon, effectively subsidizing solar. So now we might all say, 'Oh, well, solar is cost parity with coal, and solar is going to be used broadly across the world.' Well, that's true, but it's only because people dramatically accelerated the pace down the cost curve and the experience curve, and there are still plenty of innovations to be had."[4]

In addition to shifts in demographics, the new consumer class is defined by increased awareness and education. The same Deloitte study reports:

Over the past 20 years, the percentage of the population with college degrees or higher has increased significantly, though not

---

4   Harvard professor Bill Sahlman, interview with the author, September 2019.

uniformly—white and black Americans with a college education have increased by 12 percent and Hispanics by 7 percent.

As a result, we're moving toward a more educated and
knowledgeable consumer base with different spending patterns. However, the cost of education eats into discretionary
funds, influencing how consumers spend their money on categories such as apparel, food away from home, and furniture.[5]

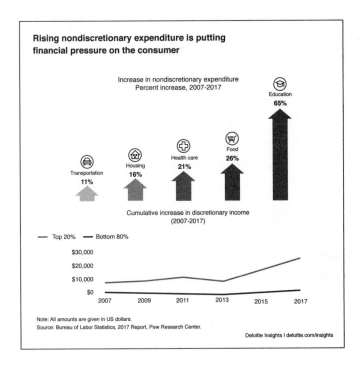

Combine this with improvements in online and communicative
technologies that benefited from a leap frog event during the COVID-19

---

5   https://www2.deloitte.com/us/en/insights/industry/retail-distribution/the-consumer-is-changing.html.

pandemic, and you are looking at a remarkably savvy marketplace. These new consumers aren't just finding the skeletons in the corporate closet; they are discovering the ones hidden under the bed and beneath the floorboards as well. In addition, these potentially corporation-killing missteps are no longer limited to gross misconduct. Elevated consumers genuinely care about issues beyond core business practices such as environmental impact and social good.

From a recent *Forbes* article:

> Accenture Strategy's Global Consumer Pulse Research revealed that consumers, across all generations, care about what retailers say and how they act.
>
> Consumers under 30—those belonging to Gen Z and Millennial generations—particularly feel a strong affiliation to retailers that subscribe to a larger purpose, according to the study of more than 2,000 UK consumers.
>
> More than six in ten younger consumers closely consider a company's ethical values and authenticity before buying their products, the research found. It represents a shift in consumer expectations of retailers.[6]

According to eBay's Kris Miller, "I do think that consumers are looking for brands that are authentic. They're looking for brands that have a purpose that aligns with their own values. That, I think, is one of the key success factors of brands and companies of the future. It's not just as consumers, it's also as employees. Employees want to work for companies who have values that are aligned with their own

---

6   https://www.forbes.com/sites/annaschaverien/2018/12/12/consumers-do-care-about-retailers-ethics-and-brand-purpose-accenture-research-finds/#44f4a82416f2.

values. They want to work for companies who have a clear, authentic purpose, that inspires them every day."[7]

Rachel Barton, managing director at Accenture Strategy, describes the consumer shift toward purpose this way:

> Five years ago, trust in a company was really that they did what they said they would. In the last few years, it has moved to trusting the foundations and purpose on which a company is built. This becomes a highly significant shift because, for many corporations in operation today, those foundations aren't exactly up to code. This combined with a massively educated, highly networked customer base [creates] a recipe for disaster.
>
> Consumers have the power to bring about success or failure to companies. They are more than buyers—they are active stakeholders and want to feel a sense of shared purpose.[8]
>
> When this sense of shared purpose is lacking, the new consumers are more than happy to hold corporate decision-making accountable. The Internet has made it simpler to see who companies actually are and then to immediately express an opinion about them.

According to the *Forbes* report about the Accenture study:

> Social media has helped to democratize the relationship between retailers and consumers, and enabled consumers to find their voice. And consumers believe it's effective: 71% of young consumers surveyed by Accenture believe that refusing to buy from

---

7 Ibid.

8 Ibid.

brands or criticizing them on social media can make a difference in how companies act.

. . . If retailers don't react, they now face consequences. More than half of Gen Z and Millennial consumers said they were likely to boycott brands that don't reflect their values and beliefs.[9]

Or, as Barton put it: "These findings should be a powerful wake-up call for all brands to become purpose-led organizations."

In addition to increasing diversity and unavoidable transparency, the new decision-making consumers of tomorrow's economy are marked by a measurable drop in expendable income. According to Nielsen, Millennial and Gen Z customers are under much heavier financial pressures at a much earlier age than those of previous generations. Or, as the study itself states:

An analysis of spending patterns of similarly aged consumers over a 30-year period reveals few significant shifts in spending allocation . . . Interestingly, the real differences show up in several non-discretionary expenditure categories. A growing share of the Millennial's wallet is going toward health care expenses, housing costs, and education, highlighting not so much a change in the consumer, but rather a change in the economic pressures that the young consumer is under.[10]

---

9 Ibid.

10 https://www.accenture.com/gb-en/insights/strategy/brand-purpose?c=strat_competitivea gilnovalue_10437228&n=mrl_1118.

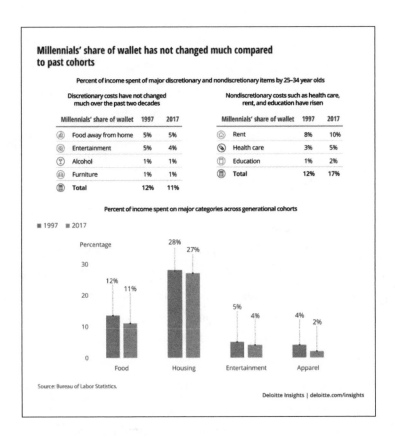

This means that not only are the economic lords of tomorrow wealthier and fewer in number than previous generations, they will also have less of that wealth to deploy on traditional commerce outside of their financial essentials. Student loans, healthcare costs, and rising costs of living in most metropolitan areas mean that consumers will still be spending more, but making fewer purchases overall. These purchases, however, may be far more traditional than many initially believed. According to Nielsen:

This observation runs counter to conventional wisdom, which posits that Millennials have shifted spending categories toward experiences and away from products . . . As far as spending patterns are concerned, today's consumer is not so different from yesterday's buyer. US retail spending has grown, but this trend has been in line with the population growth even as per capita spending remains flat . . . We must not confuse choice with change. In many ways the consumer of today is like the consumer of yesterday, they are a creature of the pressures they are under, coupled with the choices they have available to them.[11]

So, to complete the equation, the most important buying generation in history will have more wealth than any before it, but is still looking to deploy that wealth in the same way as its predecessors. New consumers still spend on food, shelter, clothes, cars, entertainment, and leisure.

We are on the verge of the most significant land grab of modern capitalism. But an alarmingly small number of people seem to have noticed. Steering around this wall requires careful technique and a practiced resolve. However, far too many leaders have yet to take their foot off the gas—they seem to think it is a straightaway.

And the results will be predictably disastrous.

THE TURN

Successfully pivoting into the Elevated Economy is potentially daunting, but taking the first step requires an understanding of what stands on the other side. Because, while the Great Wealth Migration and natural demographic trends will soon make Millennials the wealthiest and most selective buying group of all time, the risks of failure are

---

11 https://www2.deloitte.com/us/en/insights/industry/retail-distribution/the-consumer-is-changing.html.

as great as the possibilities of success. The new key consumers are just as capable of rewarding elevated companies as they are of erasing those that refuse to adapt.

The first step to accessing the rewards of the Elevated Economy is to understand that while the new consumers are a highly diverse demographic, they are rather homogeneous ideologically. The issues they care about are ones they care about very much; but that list of issues is relatively small, and the proper responses to their beliefs are relatively predictable.

A new study from economic analysis and marketing firm Cone Communications highlights the potential power of sharing the ideals of a new generation. The study used information dating back to the early 1990s to determine that today, 87 percent of customers are more willing to support companies that prioritize environmental and social good. What's most interesting, however, is that 75 percent said they would be likely to actively avoid or protest companies that don't support these causes.[12]

The potential economic opportunity is massive. If your company can be seen as "good" by its customer base, then it will be well positioned to succeed in the Elevated Economy during and following the Great Wealth Migration.

In an article concerning the Cone report by Sustainable Brands Insights, the definition of "good" for their respondents is divided into five components:

- Being a good employer

---

12 https://www.conecomm.com/news-blog/2017/5/15/americans-willing-to-buy-or-boycott-companies-based-on-corporate-values-according-to-new-research-by-cone-communications.

- Operating in a way that protects and benefits society and the environment
- Creating products and services that ensure individual well-being
- Investing in causes in local communities and around the globe
- Standing up for important social justice issues

Not one of these top five responses has anything to do with the traditional four P's of marketing (product, price, place, and promotion); in fact, there's no mention of them at all. No, the issues that are starting to matter most to new consumers are almost exclusively within the realm of that new fifth P: Purpose. Currently, it is a competitive advantage to become a purpose-driven corporation. But, as studies like this demonstrate, in just a few years that advantage will evolve into a necessity. This increases the potential for both reward and disaster—because consumers aren't the only ones paying attention.

BEYOND CUSTOMERS: ELEVATED INVESTING

It's not just customers who are being drawn into the Elevated Economy. Investors, both personal and institutional, are beginning to march in similar formations to the rapidly shifting Millennial-dominated primary consumer base of tomorrow. ESG funds are moving from niche to commonplace, with all of the functionality and marketplace pressure that goes along with such a dramatic shift in sentiment. The money in the market is beginning to have higher expectations for firms and business leaders as well.

According to *Morningstar*:

Sustainable funds in the United States attracted new assets at a record pace in 2019. Estimated net flows into open-end and exchange-traded sustainable funds that are available to U.S. investors totaled $20.6 billion for the year. That's nearly 4 times the previous annual record for net flows set in 2018.[13]

Inflows to ESG funds are likely to top $100 billion per year, and numbers that big can't be ignored. The ESG revolution is beginning to become a renaissance, even outside of funds tied specifically to its core tenets of having a positive impact on environmental, social, and governance issues; and those beliefs are manifesting themselves in more mainstream ways. Some of the largest funds around are beginning to strike a harder line with firms that aren't toeing the ESG line.

A *Bloomberg* article titled "Big Money Starts to Dump Stocks That Pose Climate Risks" begins by detailing a major rift that recently developed between ExxonMobil and one of its largest stakeholders, Legal & General Investment Management—a hedge fund that controls $1.3 trillion in assets and a top 20 shareholder for ExxonMobil. According to the article, during a particularly fraught meeting between Exxon's leadership and LGIM:

> "The Exxon delegation listened, but it didn't accept the suggestions," says [Meryam] Omi, LGIM's head of sustainability and responsible investment strategy. Around the same time, Exxon persuaded the US Securities and Exchange Commission to block a shareholder resolution that pushed the oil giant to do more to address climate risks.
>
> So, in June, London-based LGIM announced that it had dumped about $300 million worth of its Exxon shares and would

---

13 https://www.morningstar.com/articles/961765/sustainable-fund-flows-in-2019-smash-previous-records.

use its remaining stake to vote against the reappointment of Exxon Chairman and Chief Executive Officer Darren Woods.[14]

According to LGIM ESG expert Meryam Omi, "There has to be an escalation."

LGIM sold a $300 million position to send a message. And that message is: Our money is going to move, and it's going to move toward better companies, not just better investments. And LGIM is not alone in this fight.

JPMorgan continues to further its leadership position on these issues by transitioning away from investing in and financing extraction-based businesses:

> On top of stepping back from advising companies that get most of their revenue from coal extraction, JPMorgan said it will put restrictions on financing new coal-fired power plants, phase out "credit exposure" to the industry by 2024 and will stop funding new oil and gas drilling projects in the Arctic.
>
> "This new commitment is intended to address a broader set of challenges in the developing world and developed countries where social and economic development gaps persist," the bank said in a statement.[15]

UBS quickly followed suit, saying that it "would no longer finance new offshore-oil projects in the Arctic, thermal coal mines or oil sands

---

14   https://www.bloomberg.com/news/articles/2019-08-07/big-money-starts-to-dump-stocks-that-pose-climate-risks.

15   https://www.cnbc.com/2020/02/25/jpmorgan-says-it-will-fund-200-billion-in-sustainable-deals-this-year.html.

on undeveloped land as banks tighten their restrictions on fossil fuels amid pressure from environmentalists and investors."[16]

In the Elevated Economy, firms are going to face pressure on every side, from consumers all the way down. As reported by Bloomberg:

> "Momentum is gathering," says Mark Lewis, who leads climate change investment research for Paris-based BNP Paribas Asset Management. He likens it to the divestment campaign that forced companies participating in apartheid-era South Africa to change course . . .
>
> . . . But he knows it won't be easy. In March, as he helped the BNP Paribas press team put the finishing touches on an announcement that its actively managed funds would exit almost €1 billion ($1.1 billion) of coal stocks as early as next year, he thought the news might cause a few "ripples" and not much more. In fact, Lewis was bombarded with emails and calls, not all of them polite. "It surprised me how big the reaction was," he says.[17]

Change is happening at an incredible rate. The money is moving, and it's leaving many of its traditional strongholds—much to the chagrin of the commanding officers within. In a *Barron's* cover story describing America's 100 most sustainable companies, Leslie P. Norton writes:

> America's corporations are becoming more sustainable, and investors are benefiting, along with the planet and the rest of its inhabitants. The third annual *Barron's* ranking of America's

---

16 https://www.wsj.com/articles/ubs-exits-arctic-oil-coal-mines-and-tar-sands-projects-11583447745.

17 https://www.bloomberg.com/news/articles/2019-08-07/big-money-starts-to-dump-stocks-that-pose-climate-risks.

Most Sustainable Companies also makes for a pretty good port-folio: Shares of the 100 companies on our list returned 34.3% on average, in 2019, beating the S&P 500 index's 31.5%. More than half of our honorees, 55, outperformed the mighty index, which has been nearly unbeatable for a decade.

With companies in general adopting ambitious goals for their environment and workplace practices, returns will keep outperforming, predicts Calvert Research & Management, which created the ranking for Barron's. If sustainability once seemed like a hobby for a group of eccentric businesses, it's now viewed by many corporations as mission-critical.

. . . How do sustainable enterprises outperform? For one thing, they're better at personnel retention. Employee turn-over is 25% to 50% lower at these operations, studies show. Turnover among mid-level employees costs an estimated 90% to 150% of their annual salary.

In addition, good environmental policies—whether on water, facilities, fuel, or waste—can lower costs. For example, No.17-ranked Ecolab (ECL) helps restaurants, hotels and factories conserve water and save on energy by reducing hot-water usage.

Good sustainable practices are also a magnet for custom-ers, who increasingly want to show that their partners treat the environment, workers, and other stakeholders well.

"It creates a place where future employees want to work and creates significant brand value with customers," Cisco's Robbins tells Barron's.

In 2019, there was a "tipping point" in terms of companies embracing sustainability, at least as measured by a variety of envi-ronmental, social, and corporate governance, or ESG, metrics, says John Streur, CEO of Calvert, a unit of Eaton Vance (EV). "It's really rising in a meaningful way. It's evident and obvious this year in terms of the amount of information and disclosures and real progress."

. . . Calvert looked at more than 230 performance indicators that address ESG issues, such as workplace diversity, data security, and greenhouse-gas emissions. Based on the indicators, Calvert assigned a score of zero to 100 in each stakeholder category. Then, it created a weighted average of the categories for each company, based on how financially material each category was for its industry peer group. To be on our list, a company needed to be rated above the bottom quarter in each of the material stakeholder categories. If it performed poorly in any key one that was financially material, it was disqualified.

. . . At this rate of adoption, it won't be long—years, not decades—before virtually every company in America will seek sustainable advantages. [Says Calvert analyst Chris Madden]: "Companies are trying to lead their clients, suppliers, and even their competitors to become much more sustainable."[18]

Not only companies, but consumers, too, are embracing—even demanding—an Elevated Economy. Market demand is reshaping behavior at the corporate level, and once that change starts to happen, it is unlikely that those changes will ever be reversed. It's the speed of the change that is notable. Just look at the changes that resulted from the Black Lives Matter movement in the summer of 2020. As one Nielsen report puts it:

A new era of sustainability is rising, and it's touching every corner of the world. Consumers in markets big and small are increasingly motivated to be more environmentally conscious

18 https://www.barrons.com/articles/the-100-most-sustainable-companies-51581095228.

and are exercising their power and voice through the products they buy. But why do these shifts feel so urgent? There is mounting evidence to support that in many parts of the world, sustainability has become a life and death matter.[19]

This is really what makes the Elevated Economy so important. Change is happening fast and responses are dramatic; because the fifth P—Purpose—is inherently linked to issues of far greater importance than any of the other four. Buying for purpose means that people are beginning to make economic decisions through macro lenses rather than micro considerations. The concerns of the new consumers are much bigger than saving 50 cents on a pack of gum. They want to make sure the company selling that gum is working hard on more than just flavor.

Generations

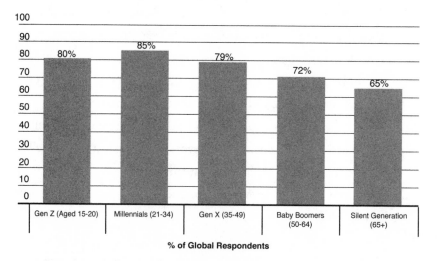

% of Global Respondents

It is extremely or very important that companies implement programs to improve the environment

---

19 https://www.nielsen.com/eu/en/insights/article/2018/global-consumers-seek-companies-that-care-about-environmental-issues/.

Elevated Consumers and Elevated Investors are demanding Elevated Companies. Making this pivot is a matter of life and death for every corporation that hopes to participate and succeed under this evolving paradigm.

Physics doesn't change. When it comes to a speeding car and a brick wall, there are only three options: you can turn, you can stop, or you can crash. In just a few short years, the CEO of every company will be faced with those same three options—turn, stop, or crash. Shifting the focus of your business from just product, price, place, and promotion to include purpose may be difficult, but the tide of change, like the laws of physics, is oblivious to these sorts of complications. As a business leader, the choice is still yours.

Don't let momentum decide your fate.

CHAPTER 3

THE NEW CONSUMERS

"If you want happiness for an hour—take a nap. If you want happiness for a day—go fishing. If you want happiness for a year—inherit a fortune. If you want happiness for a lifetime—help someone else."

—Chinese proverb

C onsumer behavior is the single most significant determining factor for corporate prosperity.

Without willing buyers, even the most innovative firm becomes irrelevant. You don't need to go to business school to come to that conclusion, but I'm often struck by how often some business leaders and analysts undervalue or outright ignore the importance of consumer behavior. Other factors are, of course, important, but none so much as the way consumers think, feel, and behave. If you want to make a successful business, what you're really trying to do is create an organization that consumers are willing to make successful for you.

No business leader has the sole power or ability to create a successful company. Their real goal is to constantly be acquiring customers. Spend any time in a country with popular outdoor markets or bazaars and you'll witness this in sharp relief. To entice shoppers, vendors shout and sing, and hassle passersby in the street. These vendors know that it may be their name on the sign, but it's those customers who are really in charge.

THE MOST IMPORTANT SHOPPERS OF ALL TIME

The new consumers of the Elevated Economy—the Internet-enabled Millennial and Generation Z beneficiaries of the Great Wealth Migration—will have more resources, more time, and more information than any other generation of consumers. The decisions they make will send shock waves throughout the global economy. Understanding these consumers, what they care about, and the ways in which they are likely to behave is the most important thing you can do to benefit from, rather than be destroyed by, the unstoppable tidal forces surrounding the Elevated Economy.

Looking back twenty years gives perspective to the amount of change the world has experienced. From the dot-com crash to September 11 to the Great Recession to the coronavirus pandemic and social justice movement, many events can shape the way we behave. McKinsey, in its recent study "The Consumer Sector in 2030: Trends and Questions to Consider," shows that almost two decades ago, 12 percent of the population owned a mobile device; that figure today is north of 60 percent. Facebook did not exist then. About a third of the world's population in developing countries was living in extreme poverty, while that number is only 15 percent now. Changes and evolutions in technology fundamentally alter the thinking and behaviors of populations. These shifts are a revolution that will forever transform the landscape.

Disruptions are normal and expected in business, but, as McKinsey is affirming, there is nothing normal or expected about the way in which this particular disruption is going to play out. The basic equations of capitalism are getting new variables, the results of which have yet to be fully understood. What we can begin to understand now, however, are the consumers themselves and the ways in which businesses may be able to stay relevant to them. But a pivot won't be enough. They will need to take completely new positions.

According to McKinsey, the Great Wealth Migration will more than live up to its title. It projects that by 2030, middle-class spending will virtually triple. In that sort of climate, the potential for new or increasingly successful firms is equally massive. However, the increase in spending does not necessarily mean it will be easier for a firm to turn all those dollars into votes that are cast in its favor. Consumers in the Elevated Economy will have more resources to deploy, but they will look at that deployment through an entirely new lens.

This lens, McKinsey says, will be forged from the multitude of issues that consumers will face and the options they will have for addressing them. The economy of 2030 will be an issue-driven, identity-centric economy. The consumers that will dominate the economy of tomorrow will still be making decisions via a fairly predictable matrix, but that matrix will contain different variables than most marketers today are using to plan their campaigns. Painting a picture of where the world will be at the turn of the next decade and how consumers behave will have several significant inputs:

- Roughly 75 percent of 2030's population of 8.5 billion will have mobile and Internet access.

- The emerging market middle class will be bigger and wealthier than their parents.

- A consumer's average age will be slightly older, because growth among aging populations in developed markets is outpacing growth in the younger demographic in emerging markets.

- Business consolidation will continue. Investors and owners are likely to be more interventionist, and firms will make use of analytics, digitization, and big data.

- Urban dwellers are increasing by 65 million every year.

- The majority of the consuming population will be centered in urban areas.[1]

McKinsey says the following five questions are key to preparing for the future:

- What makes us distinctive?

- How can we engage consumers in an ongoing dialogue?

- Are we set up to relocate resources swiftly and at scale?

- What strategic relationships should we set out to nurture?

- How can we use technology to differentiate, not just enable?[2]

When combining with other analysis and prevailing wisdom, you can create an even more focused list of three questions to see if your firm is ready to be championed by consumers of the Elevated Economy.

---

1 https://www.mckinsey.com/industries/consumer-packaged-goods/our-insights/the-consumer-sector-in-2030-trends-and-questions-to-consider.

2 Ibid.

QUESTION ONE: WHAT SHOULD OUR IDENTITY BE?

Identity is everything in the Elevated Economy. The consumers creating this rapid change in buying behavior are driven primarily by who they think they are in the world. Previous generations would make buying decisions based on their immediate needs, and these new consumers are no different—except that they have expanded the definition of what an immediate need is.

In my interview with Harvard Business School's Max Bazerman, the conversation turned to identity, and he explained the demands that society is putting on corporations through the lens of the trend toward healthy eating:

> I think that the evidence is [that] consumers are concerned about health, not that they have some moral problem with eating animals; the presumptive number of vegans and vegetarians in our land has not changed very much in the last twenty years but plant-based products are growing at 22% a year. People want to have more health in their lifestyle, as the evidence has become clearer and clearer. So, I think that's the biggest key to driving what's going on, I think society is making demands of corporations.[3]

A joint paper recently published by economics and marketing professors from the University of Pennsylvania and the University of Washington studied this phenomenon in an effort to bring some clarity and definition to these ideas on identity. According to their findings, identity in consumer behavior is a collection of five principles. They are:

---

3 Harvard professor Max Bazerman, interview with the author, October 2019.

1. **The Identity Salience Principle:** Factors that increase the salience of a particular identity within a person's self-concept will increase the probability that the identity will have a subsequent influence on the person's attitudes and behavior.

2. **The Identity Association Principle:** When stimuli become associated with a positively regarded identity, those stimuli will receive more positive evaluations and can acquire other identity-related content independent of any explicit processing of the association.

3. **The Identity Relevance Principle:** When identity information is deliberately processed, its influence will be greatest on stimuli that possess object relevance, symbolic relevance, goal relevance, action relevance, or evaluation relevance to the identity.

4. **The Identity Verification Principle:** Feedback from the external environment will be introspectively processed to determine progress toward the ideal representation of an identity.

5. **The Identity Conflict Principle:** Individuals are motivated to reduce conflict across multiple identities and can do so by managing the relative salience of their various conflicting identities.

These five principles do a good job of describing the "what" of identity-driven consumerism. The consumer begins from a place of relative salience before associating with, bringing relevance to, and verifying their identity. From there, they build systems to help that identity survive and thrive amid the constant assault of challenges and potential pivots that any identity will face. Let's put this into more real terms.

Christina moves to New York when she's 22. She's fresh out of college and just starting a career. At this point, Christina is relatively salient. As she lives through her first year in the city, Christina meets new people and has new experiences. These new variables will introduce Christina to new identities and eventually she will settle into one, or an amalgamation of several.

Let's say Christina's new friends are liberal, unmarried, have no children, and love the outdoors. As Christina self-selects these experiences and interactions, she is beginning to associate with a certain identity. Over time she will test this identity's relevance and verify that it fits her. One of the ways she will express her identity is by making purchases.

Christina is going to need new clothes, a place to live, furniture, food, entertainment, and transportation. Unlike her mother or grandmother, however, she won't be making those decisions in the aisles of a store. Christina has disposable income and access to the Internet and the most sophisticated logistical distribution system in human history. The entire world's catalogue of goods is available to her. Her choices do not have to be limited by anything other than what she wants. What the research shows us is that Christina's wants are inexorably linked to who she wants to be.

In a world where choice is virtually unlimited, the pre-existing four P's of business have diminished slightly in the shadow of the fifth. Purpose is what powers Christina's buying decisions above all else. She doesn't have to buy her new jacket from the nearest physical retail store. She can spend days researching and selecting the jacket that most closely fits the identity she's chosen. And more often than not, that product will be selected by Christina because it projects the identity that most closely resembles her own.

As the joint study explains: "Identity can be defined as any category label with which a consumer self-associates that is amenable to a clear picture of what a person in that category looks like, thinks, feels and does."[4]

One way the importance of identity is being proven is through gated offers. These are offers for deals and discounts that a company may offer if a consumer meets a certain criterion. They may need to have a certain career, or receive the code from a friend or connection. Converse has recently made headlines for its highly successful gated offers to military members and college students—two of the most frequently targeted groups for gated offers. Connecting promotions to identities has produced strong results for the company. According to a recent report on Converse's identity-driven campaigns: "A brand vision that emphasizes customer self-expression helped Converse reap nearly $2 billion in revenue in 2018. But like most categories, footwear is a crowded marketplace, and even popular brands have to fight for consumer attention."

Unlike most brands, though, Converse understands the power of personal identity. And in their search for a new approach to customer acquisition, it was that power they decided to harness:

> . . . The move fully aligns with Converse's commitment to their customers' individuality. By giving these groups an exclusive discount, the company is acknowledging that being a student or a member of the military is central to one's identity and something to honor. Members of these groups, in turn, feel truly seen and rewarded for who they are. The exchange is rich in meaning and an ideal way to launch a brand relationship.
>
> . . . Converse's gated offers give the brand direct access to lucrative markets. There are 26 million US college students who

---

4　https://www.sciencedirect.com/science/article/abs/pii/S0167811612000663.

have $574 billion in spending power, and 37 million members of the military who have $1 trillion in buying power.

And the company's strategy of using gated offers to honor students and the military will reap great rewards. Companies that implement gated offers [can] see a 3x increase in conversions and ROAS (Return On Ad Spend) as high as 20:1.[5]

With this strategy, Converse has gained much more than a healthy bottom line. By choosing to connect their products to an identity, they have also connected their company to that same identity in the minds of consumers. The students and military members who used, or even simply saw, these offers will then begin to include the brand within their identity as students and service people. And in the Elevated Economy, that is a very lucrative place to be.

An article from the *Harvard Business Review* describes this as a sort of Neighborhood Effect. Take solar panels, for example. According to the *Harvard Business Review*:

> Recent research into why people put solar panels on their houses shows very nicely how this works. You might think that their main motivation is reducing energy costs or concern for the environment. But it turns out that the strongest factor is that other solar-powered homes are near. Your neighborhood represents a powerful social identity, and it colors how you think about decisions related to your home. If you see solar panels on houses around yours, you're likely to feel that you should get them as well.[6]

---

5   https://www.sheerid.com/blog/how-converse-is-acquiring-customers-with-identity-driven-exclusive-offers/.

6   https://hbr.org/2015/01/why-your-customers-social-identities-matter.

This shows just how powerful identity is as a factor for determining consumer behavior. Electricity used to be a utility—it wasn't an industry many people thought could be disrupted. But now, expensive, invasive new solutions to long-solved problems are being adopted. They are not being adopted because of the potential savings or even the environmental impact—although these are important sub-factors. No, people are putting solar panels on their houses because their house is part of their identity. Their neighborhood is part of their identity. They want to be the type of person who would use solar panels, so they buy them.

This is such a dramatic evolution of the old Economic Man model that it should grind your long-term planning to a screeching halt. The number one question you need to be asking right now as a business leader is: What identity should we have? Not, which identity do we have? Or, which identity should we create? If you know what your customers include in their definition of their identity, it becomes relatively simple—not easy, but simple—to build a firm that reflects that identity back to them. The answer to the question "What should our identity be?" is therefore quite easy to answer. The answer is: whatever our consumer's identity already is. There are nuances, of course, but this is an important first step.

QUESTION TWO: WHAT IDENTITY ARE OUR CUSTOMERS PROTECTING?

As the fifth principle in the joint study demonstrates (the Identity Conflict Principle), by the time a consumer reaches the end of the identity-adoption process, they have reached a semi-walled state. Their goal for their identity—once they've associated with it and verified it—is to protect it. They aren't buying a Patagonia jacket just to see if it lives up to the hype; they are buying a Patagonia jacket because of how well it supports their identity as an environmentally conscious, financially successful young person. Trying to bend these identities, once formed, is ill advised, and firms that are seen as disingenuous are more likely to be labeled as threats and enemies than as saviors. Once you've decided to become an identity-driven company, the next step is to identify with as much clarity as possible which identities your key consumers are already protecting.

The Edward Lowe Foundation was founded by the late-twentieth-century business magnate (and the inventor of kitty litter) Edward Lowe. This was a man who knew something about creating products for consumers' most essential needs. His foundation had this to say about success, as it relates to identity:

> A rule of thumb to follow in developing your identity is that it should match the identity of your customers and potential customers. If you own a corporate cleaning service and are targeting Wall Street firms, you should project the conservative image of your potential customers. You might be tempted to think, "I'm not handling the money, I'm just cleaning their offices," but that would be a mistake. People like to deal with people who reflect their own image. It makes them more comfortable because they are dealing with a known entity, someone they can relate to and understand. It's important to remember that there is always a subtle, yet pervasive psychology operating as a potential customer makes a decision to buy. Although the quality of your product and service is a major factor in the outcome of the process, they judge your company by its image.[7]

---

7   https://edwardlowe.org/how-to-create-your-companys-identity/.

Those final words are more relevant now than they have ever been. In order to understand your customers, you must understand their identities. And in order for them to vote for you with their dollars, they must understand your identity.

A report from the Bucharest Academy of Economic Studies provides a succinct summary of why your company needs to understand the identities that its consumers are protecting:

> In a consumer culture people no longer consume for merely functional satisfaction, but consumption becomes meaning-based, and brands are often used as symbolic resources for the construction and maintenance of identity. All human behavior is a symbolic action. People are not just choosing the best, the fanciest, or the cheapest brands. They're choosing brands that have the right meaning. Brands are now creating value not just by the products or services they represent but by the meanings they generate. This meaning is being adopted by consumers to express who they are and what they stand for. Meaning, in fact, may be the most important product a brand creates today.[8]

In the Elevated Economy, your business's identity is the most valuable asset you have.

QUESTION THREE: HOW QUICKLY COULD WE CHANGE IF WE HAD TO?

I live in an area with earthquakes. And so, we have an earthquake plan and a stockpile of supplies. Making this plan is not my attempt

---

8   https://www.academia.edu/25722165/Consumer_Identity_and_Implications_for_the_
     Brand.

to "defeat" the earthquake. I can't. But it reminds me that I have a strategy to survive it. Right now, business leaders would do well to perform a quick audit of their organizations in order to determine just how rapidly they could change if the need arises. Because success in the Elevated Economy won't come to the firms that can fight, it will come to the ones that can adapt. And adapt quickly.

To figure out how prepared your company is to adapt, spend the time to answer the following questions:

1. What and who is my company connected to?

   If your company actively works with immoral, environmentally or socially damaging vendors or third parties, it would be wise to begin replacing those relationships today. Every connection your company has is fair game to consumers. The Elevated Economy is a very dry forest, and every eyebrow-raising connection in your corporate Rolodex is a potential spark.

2. What are the core tenets of my company?

   In a disaster, you can take only a few items with you. Even cherished heirlooms need to be left behind in favor of life-sustaining supplies like food and water. Which products, intellectual property, relationships, values, and strategies are your food and water? Identifying these early will make it easier to keep what's valuable and make the proper sacrifices when it's time to make a change.

3. What might slow my company down?

   This is an intentionally open question. If all of your customers suddenly rebelled against your most profitable product or service overnight, would you be prepared to pivot immediately? If not, why not? Are you lacking research and development resources? Are you light on working capital? Do you lack the market research to know what consumers might prefer? Think of this as a pre-mortem. How could things go wrong? If they failed, what was the cause? This is a particularly crucial time to ask the questions.

Companies in the Elevated Economy will not be allowed to operate as they have in the past. New consumers are simply too different and too powerful for those old playbooks to remain intact.

And things aren't going to start changing. They already have.

CHAPTER 4

THE AGE OF CONVENIENCE

"Life is never made unbearable by circumstances,
but only by lack of meaning and purpose."
—**Viktor Frankl**

Y ou cannot motivate someone to act against their own self-interest.

When I was running my first company in the early 2010s, our job was to connect businesses to people. Digital media wasn't what it is today, and so making that connection usually meant screaming at consumers from some flashy banner on a webpage. But not even Don Draper himself could craft an ad powerful enough to motivate a person to make a decision that acts against their own self-interest.

For example, if someone is deathly allergic to peanuts, it won't matter how clever the Skippy marketing team is; that's one customer they will never be able to convert. But the idea extends outside of physical health and well-being. A person's self-image, whether it is driven by social, emotional, or moral pressure, is just as important. A staunch liberal family in California is not going to subscribe to *Guns and Ammo* magazine. A single mom with four kids is not going to swap her minivan for a Maserati anytime soon. And although you may think no New York Yankees fan would ever buy a Boston Red Sox hat, there is one condition on which they might: to burn it.

As silly as that may seem, the idea of a sports fan buying merchandise of a rival team to destroy out of spite is a perfect example of another philosophy: a person's definition of self-interest can, and does, expand. And, if you're paying attention, you can leverage that expansion in the interests of your business.

On paper, a clothing company should never try to sell a Red Sox cap to a Yankees fan. But, if that cap could be marketed as an expression of the Yankees fan's allegiance—through its potential to serve as a burning effigy—then suddenly a connection becomes possible between a business and a consumer that on the surface didn't seem possible. A good business leader can find ways to morph his or her value proposition into the space allocated within a customer's definition of self-interest. But the best business leaders are able to create that space themselves.

As Henry Ford was building his automotive empire during the turn of the last century, he became one of the largest employers in the United States. This was the beginning of the age of mass production, and so one might think that Ford would try to squeeze every last drop of productivity he could out of his army of assembly workers. But he didn't. In fact, he did the opposite.

Henry Ford is one of the fathers of the modern workweek. The fact that the majority of jobs in the United States, and the world, are conducted during five eight-hour shifts culminating in two days off on Saturday and Sunday is in large part due to Ford and his fellow post–Gilded Age CEOs. Ford gave his employees more time off than the average factory worker received, but he didn't do so out of the kindness of his heart. He did it because he realized that his workers were also his customers.

Ford not only paid his workers enough to be able to buy one of the cars that they made, but he also realized that if his workers spent all day every day in a Ford factory, they would have no time to buy one of his cars, or, even if they did buy one, they would have no time to drive it, and then, someday buy a new one. Other business owners were having similar problems. There simply wasn't enough time in the average American worker's week to go out and spend money. And so, Ford and others like him decided to create some space. They gave their employees a two-day consecutive weekend break so that they could rest from work on one day and have enough energy to reach into their wallets on the next.

Neel Burton, M.D., reminds us in his article in *Psychology Today* that Maslow's hierarchy of needs is "a motivational theory in psychology comprising a five-tier model of human needs, often depicted as hierarchical levels within a pyramid. . . . From the bottom of the hierarchy upwards, the needs are: physiological, safety, love and belonging, esteem, and self-actualization."[1]

Good business leaders know that Maslow's hierarchy of needs is written in pen, not pencil. A human's need for food, safety, and their family's prosperity will always be more powerful than anything the sloganeers on Madison Avenue can come up with. You can only bring a customer to a buying decision if that moment of decision appears to the right person, with the right message, at the right time. As soon as your company's story puts so much as a toe across the line of what is

---

1   https://www.psychologytoday.com/us/blog/hide-and-seek/201205/our-hierarchy-needs.

not in your consumer's self-interest, it will be dismissed in one second and forgotten forever the next.

Ford and his contemporaries were able to create new definitions of self-interest for their customers. And in response, American workers started spending more. A lot more. Today, America is the number one consumer nation on earth.

Businesses can grow on the strength of a better product or service, but the biggest and most successful companies learn to appeal to the self-interest of their customers. Twitter and Facebook know that they are always one or two data breaches away from seriously jeopardizing their ability to attract and retain users. McDonald's can't charge $20 for a cheeseburger. Walmart will never become a luxury boutique. Why? Because these firms know exactly where they fit within the walls of consumer self-interest. The moment fast food stops being cheap and, well, . . . fast, it starts becoming more efficient for a consumer to fill that need elsewhere. When tech giants mishandle your private information, they become too dangerous to continue using. And when big-box stores shrink, they become too niche to provide the one-stop-shop attraction that made them so valuable in the first place.

The most important thing to understand about consumers is that they will always align with their own self-interests. But the most important thing to understand about those self-interests is that they can, and do, change. However, consumer behavior rarely changes on its own. Ford forced a change by making time a more common resource. In that environment, consumer self-interest was able to expand and Ford was waiting to slot snugly into that extra space.

Currently, we are in the middle of the largest and most aggressive change in consumer behavior since Ford invented the weekend.

THE AGE OF CONVENIENCE

Understanding the US presidential election of 2016 is key to understanding why consumer behavior and the definition of what is in our self-interest changed, what that definition looks like now, and what it's going to look like in the future. But before one can understand 2016, they have to think about what came before it.

Fifteen years before this one year changed everything, the developed world had been rocketing through the Age of Convenience. From 2000 to 2015, the Internet got bigger and the world got smaller. This gave birth to new expectations that would have sounded insane to previous generations. Computers and the Internet gave humans some very inhuman abilities. We had gained the ability to communicate and learn instantaneously. And in that type of climate, making people wait or exert themselves became a much tougher sell than it used to be. Convenience has always been one of the business world's most powerful fulcrums upon which to leverage consumer behavior (drive-throughs took off in California for a reason); but never had this convenience been in such high demand and never had the limits of that convenience been so extreme.

Fortunately for consumers, a parade of young entrepreneurs was ready to turn this hunger for convenience into the most powerful businesses in history. At the core of every FAANG (Facebook, Amazon, Apple, Netflix, and Google) company is the promise of convenience.

Google became what it is today by making information as attainable as a glass of water. Amazon brought the mall to our front door and Netflix brought the movie theater into our living room. Facebook enables us to make and maintain friendships without getting out of bed. And Apple paired all of these amazing services with equally amazing devices. The smartphone became the Colt 45 by which the Wild West of convenience was won.

The desire for extreme convenience expanded the pre-existing expectations of consumers in a major way. A luxury, once sampled, becomes a necessity.

Before 2000, it would have been madness for anyone to expect their order from the Sears catalogue to arrive in less than a week. Today, we get upset if Amazon doesn't deliver our packages in a day. Technology gave birth to new expectations and those new expectations in turn gave birth to a new set of expectations. The current ruling class of businesses were built by answering the call. But there were still those that refused to play along.

Convenience was such a powerful addition to consumers' expectations that it became almost singularly important to business success between 2000 and 2015. Amazon trounced Sears and is still giving Walmart a run for its money. It didn't matter that you could get your DVDs from the neighborhood Blockbuster; Netflix was more convenient and therefore better. People were willing to change their behavior in pursuit of convenience. And any time consumers become willing to change their behavior, there's only one thing on the horizon.

Revolution.

For a decade and a half, convenience ruled the self-interest landscape with an iron fist. After Amazon, Netflix, Facebook, and Google came the Ubers, Lyfts, Airbnbs, Instacarts, and DoorDashes of the world. These "third wave" convenience companies continue to succeed because at their core they offer their customers more convenience. This is a massive affront to the traditional business thinking of yesteryear. The cheapest product with the best quality should win in most cases. But for Instacart and DoorDash, people are sometimes paying more for an arguably worse consumer experience. But that doesn't matter. Only one thing matters: convenience. The food might be colder when it's delivered by DoorDash, but you can get it without changing out of your pajamas.

By 2015 the definition of what was in a consumer's self-interest had expanded to include this newfound ease and increased speed as components of convenience. Business leaders know that, again, a luxury, once sampled, becomes a necessity, so every business at every level was trying to provide these newest luxuries to consumers: unprecedented ease and speed. Holdouts like Toys "R" Us—which famously refused to embrace online shopping—began to not just struggle, but fold altogether. There seemed to be no stopping the Age of Convenience from rampaging through the business world for another decade and a half, but things were not what they seemed.

All of this convenience for the customer came at an expense. Underneath the hyper-efficient surface of convenience lay an ecosystem of cutthroat logistics and questionable business and labor practices. But nobody really cared. Because nobody was really looking.

Forcing companies to consider their business practices and care for all of their stakeholders would take more than a few eyebrow-raising articles in *The Wall Street Journal* about an Amazon warehouse here or a data breach there. It would take a game-changing event to galvanize these ideals.

And that event was the election of Donald Trump.

• • •

The journey of Donald Trump from reality star to US president is important to the business world for more than just tax breaks. Trump's story is symbolic of the extreme societal and sociological changes that took place in the seemingly endless cavalcade of tumult that was 2016.

The fact that a person like Trump could reach the level that he did sent a shock wave through the world.

Regardless of how you personally feel about Trump, you cannot deny that the man incites a hefty amount of controversy. You also cannot deny that moving from Barack Obama to Donald Trump created one of the most dramatic conceptual, philosophical, and political whiplashes of all time.

Examine the effects of 2016 on the three most important consumer generations of the next 50 years: the Baby Boomers, the Millennials, and Generation Z.

First, it's important to understand that Trump did not just represent Trump, the persona, he represented the last gasp of a dying phase in the culture wars. In 2015, the Baby Boomers were nearing retirement age—which also means they were about to exit the point in history where they were what the advertising world would call the "core demographic."

Simply put: the election of Trump in many ways represented a final act of dominance by a generation about to become politically, economically, and psychologically obsolete. Take a look at the poll numbers. Without Baby Boomers, or at least, white non-college-educated Boomers, there would have been no Trump presidency. His existence in office solidified what he represents to different generations. To many Boomers, he was the final paragon standing between them and a fresh wave of thinking and behavior. But to the "defeated" group—the Millennials—his presence in office represented the "victory" of something darker.

For most Millennials, 2016 was the year that sexism, racism, and xenophobia won and the social and environmental progress of the Obama years ended. For eight years, as Millennials became adults, it seemed as though the country and its economy were being leveraged in one direction, and in a single day all of that progress started to reverse. This conflict, between the ideals of two dramatically different philosophies, is the meteor that would wipe out the dinosaurs of convenience and remake the landscape of what it means to be a self-interested consumer.

Progressive thinkers became galvanized. In very sudden and dramatic fashion, the Millennial generation realized that if they wanted the world to be a certain way, they would have to take matters into their own hands. Almost instantaneously, the Trump presidency made "caring" a social imperative. President Obama—and all he represented—had lulled Millennials into a false sense of security. But Trump and 2016 quickly disabused them of that notion.

The irony in all this is that, by definition, no older generation has ever won, or can ever win, a culture war against a younger generation. The values of the next generation will always subsume the values of the previous generations—simply due to the unyielding march of time. And so, the success of Donald Trump is equal parts finale for the Boomers and inspiration for the Millennials—they weren't just angry, they were determined. And unless someone reverses the laws of nature in the next few years, they are also 100 percent unstoppable. According to a recent Nielsen study:

> In a recent global online survey, a whopping 81% of global respondents feel strongly that companies should help improve the environment. This passion for corporate responsibility is shared across gender lines and generations. Millennials, Gen Z, and Gen X are the most supportive, but their older counterparts aren't far behind.[2]

---

2 https://www.nielsen.com/us/en/insights/report/2018/the-education-of-the-sustainable-mindset/.

Sarah Landrum comments on this phenomenon in an article from *Forbes*:

> Simply put, people—Millennials most of all—want the companies they buy from to practice business sustainably and ethically. And because advertising and marketing in the States appears to have reached a deafening roar in recent years, Millennials also want companies to get serious about marketing in a socially responsible way.[3]

She goes on to enumerate from the Nielsen report that Millennials specifically want four things from companies:

- They want companies to be actively invested in the betterment of society and the solution of social problems.

- They want companies that prioritize "making an impact" on the world around them.

- They want companies to be open and honest about their efforts—and to be public about their pro-social initiatives.

- Finally, Millennials want companies to involve their customers in their good works. They want an opportunity to give back—whether it's with a gift of their time or their money.

Millennials have expanded the definition of consumer self-interest, and this has become the default definition of self-interest for an entirely new era of business. In very short order, the balance of power is going to shift from a generation that prioritized getting things

---

3   https://www.forbes.com/sites/sarahlandrum/2017/03/17/millennials-driving-brands-to-practice-socially-responsible-marketing/#c43f77d4990b.

easier, to a generation that prioritizes getting things responsibly. And the proof is in the advertising.

Big companies around the world are using their multi-million-dollar ad budgets to communicate entirely new identities to their customers. Advertising in the early 2000s focused mostly on the traditional four P's of marketing: product, price, place, and promotion. Ads today are more likely to champion a company's commitment to social change, avoiding single-use plastics, or fair-trade practices.

Generally speaking, businesses get big because they understand and leverage each generation's unique definition of self-interest, and they provide products or services that speak to that customer's identity. It's already started. There's a reason Facebook—a data company—is now trying to distance itself from its dependence on user data. There's a reason that Amazon is raising minimum wages left and right throughout its sorting facilities. There's a reason that you can now see a company's ESG scores on Yahoo Finance.

John Studzinski, vice chairman and managing director of PIMCO, speaking from the 2020 World Economic Forum (WEF), said, "ESG is something we've talked a lot about in the last couple of years and it's now becoming a tier one discussion here at Davos. We all know about 'E' [Environmental]—it's getting a lot of attention and the metrics are very clear. We know about 'G' [Governance]. If we're going to combat poverty, hunger and deal with the issues of human dignity, we've got to focus on the 'S' [Social] and be mindful of the importance of modern slavery and human trafficking in supply chains around the world."[4]

The shock of 2016 forced most Millennials and progressive Boomers to realize that if they wanted to see change, they had to be the change

---

4   https://twitter.com/BofA_News/status/1222273896306495491?s=20.

agents themselves. Suddenly, people no longer cared only about what a company could provide to them, they cared about how they provided it. The imperative to "care" is too strong to ignore. The cardinal sin of business in the previous era was failing to meet a customer's needs. In this new era that hasn't changed, but the needs of customers have.

But could this really be enough to drive such dramatic change in business? Hasn't business always operated on the fringes of morality? Won't these new customers eventually calm down, give in, and let capitalist engines run as they have for decades? Maybe, but Millennials aren't the generation that businesses should be afraid of.

Generation Z responds even more unanimously in support of ethical, elevated business practices than their Millennial predecessors. Their responses to questions like "Should businesses care about the environment/their employees/society/etc.?" are nearing 100 percent in the affirmative.

The culture wars will be won by the Millennials and Gen Z together. And these groups aren't just changing their minds, they're changing their behaviors. The revolution is already here, and it has scored its first victories—the most immediate of which is the beginning of the end of short-termism.

Short-termism is on page one of the pre-elevated economic playbook. It is the rapid and single-minded pursuit of immediate goals over long-term rewards. Short-termism is what makes environmental disasters seem "worth it" and hides the toxicity of poor governance under a veil of incremental gains. According to a recent report in the *Harvard Business Review*:

> The pressure put on CEOs to deliver quarterly results is greater than ever before. A 2014 global survey of more than 600 C-suite executives and directors, conducted by the non-profit Focusing

Capital for the Long Term (FCLT), reported that two-thirds of those surveyed said pressure for short-term results had increased over the previous five years. And short-term thinking since that survey has not abated.

. . . Many CEOs argue that they have no choice but to cave to the demands of activists and others on Wall Street to boost profits quarter after quarter. But it doesn't have to be that way. That same FCLT study also found that nearly two-thirds of those CEOs said the pressure to deliver strong short-term financial performance stemmed from their own board and their own executive team. In other words, some of the short-term thinking we're seeing is actually self-imposed, with CEOs simply getting in their own way. What makes the plague of short-term thinking somewhat puzzling is that, according to McKinsey estimates, 75% of the US market is held by buy-and-hold investors who are actually interested in the long-term value of the companies in which they've invested. Given this, you could argue that CEOs shouldn't be putting so much pressure on themselves to get strong short-term results.[5]

THE NEW CAPITALISM

Marc Benioff, the billionaire founder of Salesforce, made headlines for equating Facebook to cigarette companies and pleading with other Fortune 100 CEOs to more directly steer their firms toward elevated economic practices. Benioff calls this new mindset "The New Capitalism." In his 2004 book *Compassionate Capitalism,* he makes the case that all business leaders have an obligation to be a force for

---

5   https://hbr.org/2018/05/why-ceos-should-push-back-against-short-termism.

good. He mostly focuses on philanthropy as a force for good, but the fact that he wrote about doing well by doing good as a tech company CEO so many years ago demonstrates that this issue has been thoughtfully considered in modern tech company history before the sharp rise we've seen in the last few years in ESG and SRI.

He also set his sights on business education, claiming that business schools don't do enough to teach students to prioritize people over profits. Business schools certainly don't teach you how to care about people. They teach you how to make money. But in the Elevated Economy, this is no longer good enough; you have to be good too. Benioff was one of the first CEOs to mandate that all of his employees work from home in the early days of the coronavirus pandemic of 2020. This was just after he finished building the largest skyscraper west of the Mississippi. He had a gleaming new tower to house all his employees, but he did the right thing—led from the front—and sent everyone home two weeks before the government issued its "shelter in place" order. Benioff is good at being good, and knows his role and the leadership role he plays in the Elevated Economy.

An article in *The Economist* entitled "American Business Schools Are Reinventing the MBA" describes how professors at leading business schools were quick to agree with Benioff's ideas. "We need our students to be thoughtful about the role of business in society, particularly at a moment in time when capitalism is coming under attack," says William Boulding of Duke's Fuqua School of Business.[6]

Nitin Nohria of Harvard Business School reports how younger

---

6   https://www.economist.com/business/2019/11/02/american-business-schools-are-reinventing-the-mba.

alumni and incoming classes want "the place of work to reflect purpose and values."[7]

Jonathan Levin of Stanford's Graduate School of Business talks of business schools' responsibilities to "recognize the societal consequences of corporate actions."[8]

This should hit every current business leader like a ton of bricks. Because what this represents is the tip of a very large iceberg—underneath which lies the freezing corpse of short-termism.

Generations of very successful business leaders built their companies and their bank accounts by providing the most value they could in the shortest time possible. No CEO in 2001 would be celebrated for costing investors millions in lost productivity, by granting time off so more warehouse pickers could be home with their families for the holidays. But today, such practices can send public sentiment, stock prices, and actual profits up and to the right. Why? Because just like people, businesses act in their own self-interests. And for a business, acting in its own self-interest means acting in the self-interests of its customers. If the customers decide they're suddenly going to care, then businesses are going to have to start caring as well.

This isn't just true in the classroom; it's taking over the boardroom as well. The *Harvard Business Review* has literally changed the way it ranks its annual list of the top 100 CEOs to include elevated factors like environmentalism and fair treatment of employees. According to *HBR*:

> Since 2015, our ranking has been based not only on financial performance but also on environmental, social, and governance (ESG) ratings. For the past four years we've weighted

---

7 Ibid.
8 https://www.coursehero.com/file/53432467/Theme-1-IFM-2019pptx/.

ESG scores to account for 20% of each CEO's final ranking. This year we tweaked the formula, increasing that share to 30%. The shift reflects the fact that a rapidly growing number of funds and individuals now focus on far more than bottom-line metrics when they make investment decisions. One sign of this changing sensibility: In August 2019, 181 US CEOs who are members of the Business Roundtable signed a statement affirming that the purpose of a corporation is to serve not just shareholders but four other groups of stakeholders: employees, customers, suppliers, and communities.[9]

This change was enough to knock Amazon CEO Jeff Bezos off the list altogether. Bezos was the number one CEO on the list in 2014. This means that the richest man in the world—a man who runs a trillion-dollar market cap company—is no longer ranked among the top 100 CEOs. Not because his company isn't good at making money. But because his company needs to get better at being good.

Replacing stalwarts like Bezos in the pantheon of the business elite are moral upstarts like Walmart CEO Doug McMillon. McMillon was named the head of the Business Roundtable for the 2020–2021 term. The Business Roundtable is a highly influential collection of CEOs that includes Jeff Bezos, Jamie Dimon, and Larry Fink in its ranks. McMillon was named head of the group, based almost solely on his commitment to the principles of elevated economics. Jeffrey Sonnenfeld, senior associate dean for leadership studies at the Yale School of Management, told CNN this about McMillon's appointment: "The selection of the soft-spoken, humble, but high-performing Doug McMillon is a clarion call of the US business community

---

9   https://hbr.org/2019/11/the-ceo-100-2019-edition.

endorsing the wise position that doing good is not antithetical to doing well. [McMillon has been a] bold, influential advocate for responsible society engagement."[10]

As the Harvard rankings demonstrate, it has already fallen out of fashion to value "profits over people," but it is quickly becoming a risk to the bottom line as well.

According to a podcast from *HBR*:

> Hiro Mizuno, CIO of GPIF, the Japanese Government Pension Investment Fund, one of the largest pools of capital in the world, integrates Environmental, Social and Governance (ESG) issues into every aspect of GPIF's portfolio. Mizuno believed the only way to meet his responsibilities to his beneficiaries was to improve the performance of the entire economy by improving corporate governance, increasing inclusion and gender diversity, and reducing environmental damage from climate change.[11]

A shift from generating short-term shareholder value to long-term global economic longevity is currently being pitched to business leaders everywhere. There is no longer a world in which a company can, without consequence, actively damage the environment, lack diversity at the board level, or treat its stakeholders poorly and still thrive. The advent of awareness about the health consequences of smoking placed a permanent limit on the tobacco industry. Millions of people still smoke, but the industry is a shadow of what it once was and will never return to its former glory. The drama of 2016,

---

10   https://www.cnn.com/2019/09/19/business/doug-mcmillon-walmart-ceo-business-roundtable/index.html.

11   https://hbr.org/podcast/2019/08/should-a-pension-fund-try-to-change-the-world.

the emergence of Millennials and Gen Z as the new consumer, and the rapidly pivoting mindsets of the world's business leaders all add up to one thing: change.

Or, as Joe Biden put it in an op-ed for *The Wall Street Journal*:

> Short-termism—the notion that companies forgo long-term investment to boost near-term stock price—is one of the greatest threats to America's enduring prosperity. The country can't unlock its true potential without encouraging businesses to build for the long-run.[12]

Consumer behaviors are changing because consumers themselves have changed. The revolution has begun and the money is already moving. Now the only question is: Are you ready to move with it?

The Age of Convenience is over. The Age of Elevated Economics has taken its place.

---

12   https://www.wsj.com/articles/how-short-termism-saps-the-economy-1475018087.

CHAPTER 5

THE DAY THE
SHAREHOLDERS DIED

*"I would rather die a meaningful death than to live
a meaningless life."*

—Corazon Aquino

hy do people make purchases?

Homo economicus—or, as the legendary nineteenth-century economist John Stuart Mill referred to him, the Economic Man is an odd creature. As his prehistoric moniker would suggest, the Economic Man is meant to represent how a human would react to the economy if he were completely rational—as if his brain were replaced with a calculator.

When presented with a multitude of options, the Economic Man should always choose the option that maximizes personal utility—the one that is the cheapest, easiest, and most conducive to his own personal thriving, with no regard for anyone else. Economic Man never shops anywhere but Walmart, and he flees from high-end boutiques as if they were a charging woolly mammoth.

Mill and his contemporaries used the Economic Man theory as a mental construct by which to measure brutal capitalist principles as the United States careened into the Gilded Age. The Economic Man believes that businesses, products, and the economy itself are only useful to humans as a means of improving their own individual existence. This applies to businesses as well.

The role of business in the Economic Man model is to win a constant and ruthless race to the bottom. Customers in this model are not expected to purchase more expensive products, because that depletes their resources more than is necessary. They will not travel farther or think longer than is necessary. Products are not personal. Services are not frivolous. This business model is about one thing: maximizing utility.

As the Gilded Age set in during the 1870s, the Economic Man model reigned supreme. Businesses cut costs for consumers and raised margins for themselves at an incredible rate by adopting a blatant disregard for ethical business practices, which helped line the pockets of major industrialists like Standard Oil and Gould's railroad companies. Carnegie Steel is largely exempted from inclusion in this category, because of the enlightened philosophy of its founder.

In his 1901 book *The Gospel of Wealth and Other Timely Essays*, Andrew Carnegie charged the wealthy to engage in philanthropy to better the lives of the less fortunate instead of living ostentatiously, leaving money to heirs, or leaving money to charity in their wills. In his lifetime, Carnegie donated $350 million to charity, most notably for libraries and universities. He prefigured the Elevated Economy by over a century. According to the Philanthropy Roundtable:

Andrew Carnegie may be the most influential philanthropist in American history. The scale of his giving is almost without peer: adjusted for inflation, his donations exceed those of virtually everyone else in the nation's history. The magnitude of his accomplishments is likewise historic: he built some 2,811 lending libraries around the globe, founded what became one of the world's great research universities, endowed one of the nation's most significant grant makers, and established charitable organizations that are still active nearly a century after his death. And, perhaps uniquely among businessmen, the quality of his writing has ensured that his thoughts on philanthropy have been continuously in print for more than a century, and remain widely read and studied to this day.[1]

Carnegie aside, America had a remarkable tolerance for unethical practices while they were happening. The nation was still more than a half century away from FDR and the New Deal and, by Economic Man standards, everything was humming along as planned. After all, as thought leaders like Mill wrote during this time, "It is not from the benevolence of the butcher, the brewer, or the baker that we expect our dinner, but from their regard to their own interest."

Today, we cringe to think that these practices and philosophies were ever part of the American economic landscape, and yet we often forget that change is a constant, that the economic values of today will by no means be the economic realities of tomorrow. The only constant in business is change.

---

1 https://www.philanthropyroundtable.org/almanac/people/hall-of-fame/detail/andrew-carnegie.

As 1800 became 1900, the scars of the Civil War began to heal, and aggressive westward expansion dramatically increased the strength of the US economy. During this time, its citizens were suddenly faced with something they weren't completely prepared for: disposable income and the new options it provided. A more prosperous society began to redefine what it meant to "survive" in this new growing economy. As the 1800s drew to a close, new companies and new trends began to emerge, and by the mid-twentieth century, concepts like "convenience," "luxury," and "lifestyle" began to seep into our collective economic mindset. Middle-class wealth and material accumulation began to emerge, and by the time of the post-WWII economic boom, the idea of happiness began to be conflated with wealth and possessions until the stark consumerism of the 1980s eventually equated Life, Liberty, and the Pursuit of Happiness with life, liberty, and the pursuit of a two-car garage.

In fact, the middle class, which first began to emerge as a result of the Industrial Revolution and gained momentum thereafter, has grown smaller every decade since 1970.

According to a study released by NPR, the year 2015 marked the first year that the middle class was no longer a majority demographic in the United States.[2]

Still, in mid-century America, the Economic Man had evolved. He'd left his Cro-Magnon ways behind to embrace new ideals that a cadre of contemporary economists would dub "Behavioral Economics." As money and options increased, those paying attention in the middle to late 1900s realized that humans were buying for more than just survival. They were buying to imbue themselves with social status, to support causes, and to augment their sense of self.

---

2 https://www.npr.org/2016/07/05/481571379/a-brief-history-of-americas-middle-class.

Luminaries in the study of behavioral economics include Nobel laureates Gary Becker (motives, consumer mistakes; 1992), Herbert Simon (bounded rationality; 1978), Daniel Kahneman (illusion of validity, anchoring bias; 2002), and George Akerlof (procrastination; 2001).

Their thinking began to align much more closely with Mill's precursors: Thomas Jefferson, John Locke, and even Aristotle. Behavioral economics, for the first time, included the perception and experience of others as a principal motivating force when it comes to making purchases and driving consumer behavior. Or, as the Center for Civic Education would put it:

> Locke, Jefferson, and others learned from ancient philosophers, especially Aristotle, that these choices have ethical or moral dimensions: those without moral virtue cannot be happy. Many of our choices have social consequences and therefore have a civic dimension when they enhance or subtract from "public happiness." Thus "The Pursuit of Happiness" must refer both to public and to private happiness.[3]

Business has laws, just like physics. Chief among them is this: no business can motivate a person to act against his or her own self-interest.

However, what a business can attempt to do is to expand the definition of self-interest. If the definition of what it means to act in one's self-interest is expanded to include not just the consumer but also all stakeholders related to the transaction about to take place, a new opportunity is created. An opportunity for the business to tell the consumer who they are, not just what they sell. We all want to be treated well in our work. We all want to breathe clean air and enjoy

---

3   https://www.civiced.org/resources/curriculum/911-and-the-constitution/terms-to-know.

the great outdoors. We all want to know our children, our grand-children, and our great-grandchildren will have better lives than we did. This is how the new definition of "self-interest" was beginning to expand as we entered the new millennium.

The definition of self-interest has grown to include the environ-ment, fair treatment of employees and vendors, a clean supply chain, a socially responsible enterprise, support for the local community, and efficient plant and equipment. The new definition of self-interest is no longer simply the Economic Man deciding what is good for only himself; it is a more nuanced, thoughtful consideration of every stake-holder related to the transaction.

The world and its consumers have always marched toward evolving values. Today, it's no different: the Economic Man has evolved yet again. He has moved past behavioral economics and into a new era. His voice now comes not only from consumers demanding change, but from the likes of Blackrock CEO Larry Fink, who, as noted earlier, wrote that:

> To prosper over time, every company must not only deliver financial performance, but also show how it makes a positive contribution to society. Companies must benefit all of their stakeholders, including shareholders, employees, customers, and the communities in which they operate. Without a sense of purpose, no company, either public or private, can achieve its full potential. It will ultimately lose the license to operate from key stakeholders. It will succumb to short-term pressures to distribute earnings, and, in the process, sacrifice investments in employee development, innovation, and capital expenditures that are necessary for long-term growth.[4]

---

4   https://www.nytimes.com/interactive/2018/01/16/business/dealbook/document-BlackRock-s-Laurence-Fink-Urges-C-E-O-s-to-Focus.html?dlbk.

Fink calls this shocking statement "The New Paradigm." Take a moment to contrast this with Mill's preceding words. If they had a time machine, those butchers, brewers, and bakers would be sweating behind the thin veneer of self-interest that served them so well over a century ago. Today's reality is proving yesterday's ideas wrong. Our default position toward purchases is no longer purely selfish, it is one of consideration—for all the stakeholders.

The house of cards that was the old economic paradigm has already started to fall. The tipping point has already come and gone. It happened on August 19, 2019, at 9 AM. Or, as I call it, the Day the Shareholders Died:

August 19, 2019

For the past two decades, the official stance of America's top corporate executives has been that the interests of shareholders come before the interests of all others—workers, consumers, the cities and towns in which their companies operated, and society as a whole. Today, that changes.[5]

This is the lede from a *Fast Company* article published on August 19, 2019. It bears the headline "America's top CEOs say they are no longer putting shareholders before everyone else."

The United States is the most ambitious and successful capitalist experiment ever conducted. If Moses had gotten his commandments from the business titans of the past century, there would only be one commandment: maximize shareholder value. So, this statement from this particular group shocked a lot of professionals to their core.

For centuries, market forces have produced controversial but

---

5 https://www.fastcompany.com/90391743/top-ceo-group-business-roundtable-drops-shareholder-primacy.

impressive results. The United States is the world's leading economic power. It is the cornerstone of the world economy. The dollar remains the most important economic invention in human history. And despite constant competition and strengthening rivals in the East, the grand experiment of the United States has paid off.

Some of the responsibility of continuing this experiment has passed to the members of the Business Roundtable, a group composed of the United States' most influential CEOs. Its roster boasts several business hall-of-famers, including the heads of Amazon, Apple, Boeing, FedEx, GE, PepsiCo, Visa, and pretty much every other American CEO of note.

Its official mission is to promote "a thriving US economy and expanded opportunities for all Americans through sound public policies."

The order is important here. The Business Roundtable exists *primarily* to ensure that the US economy thrives. And this is the group that just delivered its Statement on the Purpose of a Corporation to the world. Here is the eye-popping new definition from the Roundtable:

> While each of our individual companies serves its own corporate purpose, we share a fundamental commitment to all of our stakeholders. We commit to:
>
> Delivering value to our customers. We will further the tradition of American companies leading the way in meeting or exceeding customer expectations.
>
> Investing in our employees. This starts with compensating them fairly and providing important benefits. It also includes supporting them through training and education that help develop new skills for a rapidly changing world. We foster diversity and inclusion, dignity and respect.

Dealing fairly and ethically with our suppliers. We are dedicated to serving as good partners to the other companies, large and small, that help us meet our missions.

Supporting the communities in which we work. We respect the people in our communities and protect the environment by embracing sustainable practices across our businesses.

Generating long-term value for shareholders, who provide the capital that allows companies to invest, grow, and innovate. We are committed to transparency and effective engagement with shareholders.[6]

To put this in context, the 1977 iteration of this same group stated that "the paramount duty of management and of boards of directors is to the corporation's stockholders." Today, that same "paramount duty" comes dead last after delivering customer value, investing in employees, and sustaining ethical supply chains.

How? How did the entire playbook change in less than 50 years? How did we go from championing shareholder value to reducing it to an afterthought? The answer doesn't come from corporations. It comes from the people. The customers. The people are shaking Mt. Olympus. And the gods are getting restless. Or, as one *Inc.* magazine headline puts it, "In This Single Statement, CEOs from the Largest US Corporations Just Changed the Purpose of Business."

As it turns out, the Economic Man model did get one thing right: consumers and businesses do act in their own self-interest. And for businesses, self-interest means producing products and services that customers will actually pay for. This means becoming more than a

---

6   https://www.businessroundtable.org/business-roundtable-redefines-the-purpose-of-a-corporation-to-promote-an-economy-that-serves-all-americans.

company with good products at fair prices. It means becoming a company with good values and fair practices.

Some companies have been doing this well since their inception. And others are grinding their gears as they try to upshift to adapt to rapidly evolving consumer behavior. Still others are on their way to crashing altogether. The new era of elevated economics will have its winners and its losers.

DON'T BUY THIS JACKET

Like any major upheaval, the transition to elevated economic practices has signals, first movers, and early adopters. But even a cursory glance at the current business landscape will show you that that nascent momentum is slowly being replaced by sustained velocity.

I live in the San Francisco Bay Area. It's the land of the $9 coffee, where Teslas roam free. This great land of fog and silicon has a uniform. Spend any amount of time wandering the streets of San Francisco, Oakland, or Marin County and you're bound to spot more than a few people donning sleek, lightweight windbreakers, micro-puff jackets, or warm fleeces—all emblazoned with the same unmistakable logo: Patagonia.

Patagonia makes outdoor gear that services the Bay Area's residents' seemingly insatiable enjoyment of the outdoors—or at least the insatiable appetite to *seem* like they enjoy the outdoors. Walk into any Patagonia store and you'll see humble racks of muted blues, earthy brown-yellows, and brilliant reds sporting $200, $300—even $500 price tags.

On many of these garments you'll find tags lauding the company's commitment to fair trade sewing and the company's pledge that one percent of its revenue goes to protecting and restoring our planet. You

don't find tags like this on Gucci belts or Prada bags, and the reason
for that is simple: A lot of people don't actually buy a Patagonia to
go hiking. They buy Patagonia to tell the world—and themselves—
something important.

The price and branding strategies of Patagonia communicate a
subtle but consistent message: you, as our customer, should want to
pay for quality goods, keep them for as long as you possibly can, and
continue to make buying decisions that act in the interests of laborers,
suppliers, vendors, employees, and the environment. These philosophies have made Patagonia gear the ultimate way that consumers can
express their environmentalist, conservationist, socially conscious,
and yes, affluent identities.

Patagonia believes so much in its
mission that its founder and CEO,
Yvon Chouinard, at one point ran
advertisements that literally asked
consumers not to buy the jackets his
company makes.

The "Don't Buy This Jacket"
Campaign featured simple pictures
of Patagonia jackets alongside lists of
all the ways a customer's current garment could be repaired if it needed
to (Patagonia has offered free repairs
since its earliest days) and also several
sustainable ways for new customers
to obtain previously owned coats for
their next adventure.

Chouinard's argument is that a
jacket should cost a few hundred

bucks and last a lifetime—instead of being a progressively cheaper fashion statement that you replace every few years. And the market is voting in favor of that argument every single day. Chouinard realized that manufacturing *anything* hurts the planet, and so he has structured his company to be as responsible as it can possibly be. Even the company's mission statement has changed to something more direct, urgent, and crystal clear: "Patagonia is in business to save our home planet."[7] And this message is winning over customers left and right, both in the Bay Area and around the world.

Why? Because Patagonia is not selling primarily jackets. Its real product is the opportunity to communicate an identity. By sporting that logo, a consumer gets the opportunity to silently raise his or her hand in support of quality, ethics, fairness, and the environment. And, more importantly, they have an opportunity to broadcast that support to the communities they care about. The true business of Patagonia is self-expression, and business is very good. Chouinard's personal net worth is $1.5 billion, and his company does more than $750 million in annual sales.

Despite its success, Patagonia has long been seen as a corporate outsider, a dissident, a defiant individualist. It has had to endure rolling eyes and dismayed glances from traditional competitors pursuing traditional production, sales, and marketing tactics. However, it is now seeing its previously unique sentiments copied, echoed en masse by the rest of corporate America.

Patagonia may have been one of the first to prioritize values and ESG (environmental, social, and governance) practices into its supply chains, marketing, and customer relationships, but it won't be the last.

---

7   https://www.fastcompany.com/90280950/exclusive-patagonia-is-in-business-to-save-our-home-planet.

The market's increased willingness to pay for products and services coming from identity-focused businesses and identity-focused marketing has become too great for larger companies to resist.

THE EARLY ADOPTERS

The Colonel wants to sell less chicken.

It was recently announced that Kentucky Fried Chicken—one of the most iconic franchises in America—will begin rolling out experimental menu items that contain no chicken. Instead, the fast casual juggernaut's crisp, oily signatures will be recreated with plant-based alternatives.

This is not an isolated incident. Burger King also tested plant-based beef in several test markets and then launched the option across the United States. Starbucks is working hard to develop ethical supply chains within its own complex network of global coffee farmers and roasters. And Nike, yes, THAT Nike, is now viewed as the most sustainable apparel company in America, according to a recent survey conducted by CGS (Computer Generated Services).

Less than two decades ago, Nike was seen as one of the corporate world's biggest moral offenders. In 1991, activist Jeff Ballinger published a report documenting low wages and poor working conditions at one of the shoe giant's Indonesian production facilities. From then on, a string of further accusations, scandals, and revelations sparked a new American conscience about Nike's labor practices.

For most of its history, the garment industry has continuously relied on cheap labor to drive down costs and boost margins—and for a long time everyone knew exactly where to get it: within less regulated foreign markets such as China, Indonesia, India, Pakistan, and Vietnam, to name a few. Nike, Apple, and other massive consumer goods companies have faced controversy after controversy over their overseas labor practices. If Upton Sinclair were still alive, he'd have written a sequel to *The Jungle* called *Foxconn*.

However, after a generation of losing the information wars to investigative journalists, Nike did something big: it changed. Eighteen years after Ballinger's report, a consistent stream of enhancements to its supply chains, labor relations and practices, environmental initiatives, and corporate governance has allowed Nike to virtually erase its sweatshop label and trade in its bloodstained swoosh for one of purest green.

This is the same Nike that ran ads honoring Colin Kaepernick two years before the Black Lives Matter movement gained momentum in 2020. Kaepernick drew attention to social injustice by kneeling during the national anthem prior to playing in professional football games. This cost him his job, but Nike stuck by his side. Perhaps they learned their lesson from their earlier mistakes.

In 2019, CGS conducted its annual US Consumer Sustainability Survey. In it, consumers were asked which apparel company they viewed as being the most environmentally friendly. Surprisingly, Nike topped the list at number one. That type of mindshare in the marketplace would have been unthinkable for the brand even five years ago, and it stands as a testament to the millions of dollars the company has spent on changing its behaviors and communicating those behaviors to the world.

A small boutique can build a business based on ethical sustainability today without batting an eye, but Nike was founded in 1964. A tiger that old will only change its stripes if it has to. And today, the call for the corporate world to change is coming from where it has always come from: the next generations.

Over two-thirds of the consumers polled said that they give sustainability serious consideration when making their everyday buying decisions. Nearly 70 percent said that sustainability is at least "somewhat important" to them when making a purchase, and 47 percent would pay more for a sustainable product. But as the respondents get younger, those numbers get even higher.

According to the study, members of Generation Z are willing to pay 50 to 100 percent more for a product if they know it comes from a sustainable source. By the end of 2019, this had become the most populous generation in the United States—encompassing over 32 percent of the country's citizenry.

No matter what field you are in, 70 percent of anything is a statistic that jumps off the page. These numbers are well past the level that could be cited as merely a trend or temporary spike. This is a sustained change in behavior. This is a complete and total revolution.

And it is showing no signs of slowing down.

THE NEW GOLDEN METRIC

To borrow a turn of phrase from Theodore Parker, Abraham Lincoln, and Martin Luther King Jr.—I believe that the arc of consumer behavior, over time, will bend toward the just. That when given the time, resources, and opportunity, human beings as a whole will take actions that improve not just their own lives, but the lives of their neighbors, families, the environment, and future generations as well.

Alexei Agratchev, CEO of RetailNext—a global retail analytics firm—studies these trends. And his findings indicate that consumers are indeed on the move. Their destination is more efficient buying from more sustainable corporations. In an interview, Agratchev explained to me that:

> One of the biggest shifts in consumer behavior over the last 20 years, is, if you look at almost every aspect of our lives, from the way we download or listen to music, the way we listen to

video, the way we take and share pictures, the way we order transportation like we do, by the way we find places to stay and exercise—everything's been impacted by technology in these dramatic ways—you can't recognize the way you do most of these things today compared to 20 years ago.

Billions and billions of people go into retail stores every year, but it really hasn't changed that much until recently. The experience when you go into a department store or a grocery store today or 50 years ago, a lot of the experience has been the same. And I think that's part of the reason that led to a lot of these guys doing very badly, because people expect things to be better, and the retail industry was behind. And I think the brand industry is behind. The way they manufacture things, the way they deliver things.

. . . I think people feel like they need to show that they are doing more than just focusing on profits. "As long as that is within the law, we'll do whatever we need to maximize profit." That's been the general mood, but I see that changing.[8]

This change is happening now on a larger and more significant scale than anything we have ever seen. The result of this is a tectonic shift in not just how firms do business, but what it means to be in business altogether. Specifically, this change boils down to one thing: for the first time in the history of capitalism, it has become best practice to prioritize stakeholders over shareholders.

In business, you need a golden metric. A single number you can use to measure the success of all the many strategies and initiatives you and your team are cranking out, year after year. For most of this

8 Alexei Agratchev, CEO of RetailNext, in discussion with the author, December 2019.

nation's history, that metric for its most successful businesses was share price. If a business is healthy overall, it logically should be able to generate value for those who invested their hard-earned money in it.

However, the Business Roundtable's call to arms—and dozens of other headlines popping up every day from CNBC to the *Journal*—indicate that the golden metric has shifted. Today, being a healthy business that consumers will pay for does not mean creating value for just its shareholders. It means creating value for all its stakeholders. And it means rethinking who belongs in that group to begin with.

Previously, stakeholders were shareholders. Today, however, that list has grown to include the community, suppliers, vendors, consumers, and the environment. This demand is coming from consumers. And, as any good economist will tell you, demand will always hold more importance in our economy than any other force. Remember that Nielsen study:

> Nearly half (48%) of US consumers say they would definitely or probably change their consumption habits to reduce their impact on the environment. And these consumers are putting their dollars where their values are, spending $128.5 billion on sustainable fast-moving consumer goods (FMCG) products this year. Since 2014, these influential shoppers have grown sustainable product sales by nearly 20%, with a compound average growth rate (CAGR) that's four times larger than conventional products (3.5% vs −1.0% comparatively). By 2021, we expect these sustainably minded shoppers to spend up to $150 billion on sustainable FMCG goods.[9]

---

9   https://www.nielsen.com/us/en/insights/article/2018/was-2018-the-year-of-the-influential-sustainable-consumer/.

The market is demanding products and services from sustainable, ethical, conscientious companies that treat their people well, protect the earth, and commit to working toward a healthier future. Or, as Nielsen again surmises:

> Corporate responsibility and sustainability strategies may take different shapes around the world, but one thing is clear: consumers are using their spending power to effect the change they want to see. This isn't a trend a company can simply sidestep. Sooner or later, whether through government regulation, sheer force of nature, or public outcry, companies will need to respond. No matter what market you're in, connecting sustainability factors to how it impacts consumers is the key.[10]

This is the new market—one that is increasingly dominated by values, not value. And while there are many things a business can control, the market itself is not one of them. Especially not this one.

But that hasn't stopped some from trying, and failing, to spectacular effect.

---

10   Ibid.

CHAPTER 6

THE FOURFOLD FOUNDATION

"Lost time is never found again."
—Benjamin Franklin

Combat is common in business.

In the '80s and '90s it was the "Personal Computer Wars" between Apple, IBM, and Dell. Then came the "Smartphone War" in the 2000s between Apple and Samsung. And more recently, we entered the era of the "Streaming Wars" between Netflix, Amazon, Hulu, HBO, and others.

But then, a new combatant stepped into the arena: Disney launched its streaming service in late 2019, bringing its immense catalogue of content to smartphone screens around the world.

For $6.99 per month, Disney+ offers its users a catalogue of Disney's animated and live-action films and television shows, as well as those produced by Lucasfilm (*Star Wars*), Marvel Entertainment (The Marvel Cinematic Universe), ESPN (Sports), and National Geographic (Nature and Documentaries). A trailer showing just a few seconds from every piece of streamable content offered by Disney+ clocked in at just over three hours long. That's a lot of content. And it isn't cheap. According to *Variety*, Disney will spend over $1 billion to produce original content for its new streaming service—a figure that rises to over $2.5 billion by 2024. The truly interesting thing about Disney is not how much money it is putting into the project, it's how much effort it is devoting to it, and what this new service means for Disney as a business.

For decades, Disney's business model has been relatively straightforward: get people to get in their cars, drive to a theater or a theme park, pay for a ticket, and enjoy the experience. Ticket and merchandise sales are the bread and butter for the folks in Burbank. And yet, on the eve of a new decade, Disney decided to devote huge amounts of focus and manpower to launch a service that, for many years, was considered antithetical to its core business, and just in time for the coronavirus to force us all into our homes. Regarding COVID-19, Disney was "in a unique position because nearly every aspect of its business is exposed—from the parks division, which brings in more than a third of Disney's revenue, to television," writes Dylan Byers of NBC News.[1]

When Netflix popularized online streaming for traditional media (e.g., film and television), the pundits were quick to point out the looming threat that its progress posed to the incumbent entertainment powerhouses. The stage seemed set: Netflix and its ilk were going to do everything in their power to get you to subscribe, while traditionalists like Disney were going to lock their big-budget spectacles behind paywalls guarded by ticket takers.

Surely the house that Walt built would be able to go toe to toe

---

1   https://www.nbcnews.com/news/all/disney-its-new-ceo-face-major-challenge-coronavirus-pandemic-n1165161.

with Netflix and come out on top. But instead of fighting Netflix, Disney became Netflix. Why not fight the good fight and vanquish this new young rival? The answer is that the real battle is not a battle between Netflix and Disney, it's a battle for us. The real war isn't Apple vs. Microsoft or Google vs. Facebook. The real battle is corporations vs. the attention of consumers. And Disney has been around far too long not to know the difference.

The conversations happening at Disney were not "What are we going to do about Netflix?" They were "What are we going to do about this change in consumer behavior?"

Bob Iger, former CEO, now executive chairman of the Walt Disney Company, took the time to understand the desires of Disney's customers, and then put in the effort to meet those consumers where they were. Customer centricity is a term used in Marketing 101. Because when you put the customer at the center of everything you do, you win. Disney might be big, but it knows that the will of the customer is bigger. Always has been. Always will be. And adaptable companies like Disney are going to reap the rewards.

Judo Strategy is another core principle employed by CEOs and strategists all over the world. David Yoffie, one of my most admired professors, has been teaching it for over 20 years. He literally wrote the book on it: *Judo Strategy: Turning Your Competitors' Strength to Your Advantage.*

Analysts projected that by the end of 2019, around two months after Disney+ launched, the new service would be able to scrape together around 8 million paying subscribers. On day one, the company announced that it had signed up over 10 million subscribers. True business "combat" is not boxing. It's not always about knocking out your competition. In reality, the real "wars" of business are fought with judo. It's about taking the size and weight of your opponent and using it to flip them so you are left with greater profits. Judo is designed for smaller opponents to beat larger ones, and it's important to remember that it's the consumers, not corporations, who really control the outcome of all these "fights."

Succeeding in business is an exercise in consistent humility. You may lead your business, but you do not control it. That power lies with your consumers. The Disney example is specific: very few firms out there will make their millions in the online streaming space, but it's Disney's mindset that business leaders should hope to emulate.

As the Elevated Economy steps more firmly into the spotlight, many businesses have already begun scrambling to update their identities and value propositions to earn the dollar-votes of consumers who suddenly care. The adjustments will be different for every firm, but on the macro level there are four cornerstones that every company must incorporate if it hopes to survive and thrive in the Elevated Economy.

Netflix may have signaled to Disney when consumers began to care about convenient content consumption, but now the Elevated Economy is showing all companies that consumers are beginning to care. About everything.

CORNERSTONE ONE: DIVERSITY AND INCLUSION

The cornerstones of elevated firms are indifferent to product, service, location, business vertical, or years in business. Every business must take heed if it wants to thrive among the rapidly emerging changes in consumer behavior we are seeing today.

If you have the ability to advocate for these changes, the time has come to spring into action. Begin with diversity and inclusion.

The basics need to be clarified. You aren't an elevated company just because everyone on your payroll hates their managers equally.

An important subsection of the definition for diversity and inclusion needs to be that all employees and stakeholders have equal abilities to thrive, not just that they have equal access to roles and upward mobility.

An excerpt from a story printed in *The Telegraph* zeroes in on the definitions and importance of diversity and inclusion in the modern economy:

> Put simply, diversity can be seen as a means of differentiating people from one another, through dimensions such as ethnicity, gender, nationality, age, disability, sexual orientation, education or religion. But Farrah Qureshi, the chief executive of the Global Diversity Practice (GDP), says that it's much more than this.
>
> "It's about respecting and appreciating our differences," she explains. "The key question for companies is how to leverage those diverse perspectives, lifestyles, and backgrounds to drive business success and innovation."[2]

Qureshi adds that in an era when firms face complex challenges and geopolitical shifts, diversity is seen as an enabler—a way to succeed in an evolving marketplace. It's fast becoming a strategic priority.

The benefits of diversity in business are many, but leaders should be careful of falling into "tokenism," or the belief that the presence of a diverse staff will inevitably bring the benefits of a truly unbiased workplace. Inevitably, employees must be motivated by larger, shared goals rather than individual compensation. As eBay's Kris

---

2   https://www.telegraph.co.uk/connect/better-business/business-sustainability/business-benefits-diversity-inclusion/.

Miller puts it: "I do think the reason why many people here at eBay come to work for eBay and stay at eBay, is because they really do appreciate helping people."[3]

The goal cannot be just to build multicultural or multiethnic teams. The priority has to be intentionally and consistently creating systems and pathways by which every person in a company has equal access to success and an equal chance to thrive. When that happens, according to research compiled by TalentLyft—featuring studies from the *Harvard Business Review* and other managerial thought leaders—there are direct internal benefits that come from having a diverse and inclusive workplace. These benefits are: a variety of useful perspectives, increased creative performance, higher levels of measurable innovation, faster problem-solving capabilities, better decision-making capabilities, higher levels of employee engagement, reduced employee turnover, more effective hiring, and increased profits.

That's a list of improvements that any company would be happy to achieve, but in the Elevated Economy the benefits of a diverse and inclusive workplace go beyond internal benefits. The external identity that a diverse and inclusive company is able to communicate is arguably more valuable than all of those internal improvements put together. In the Elevated Economy, consumers are looking to support companies they care about. And those consumers will care more about companies that care about diversity and inclusion.

Diversity and inclusion are dual foundational elements of an elevated business. If you are at a company that has no intentional or proactive plans in place to address and cultivate this type of success, alarm bells should already be ringing. Because there aren't only benefits to be gained, there is a lot to lose as well.

---

3 Miller, discussion with author.

Diversity and inclusion have been historically complex for even the most progressive companies to get right. Recently, a cadre of African American Facebook employees made headlines when they released an anonymized collection of racially motivated disadvantages plaguing the social media giant's inner workings. The response from Facebook was swift and promises for change were forthcoming, but the damage was done. Management was on the offensive, and the company's ability to attract and retain diverse talent was called into question.

Those bells can't be unrung.

CORNERSTONE TWO: PAY EQUALITY

Businesses are, by nature, creatures of finance. Their existence revolves around generating revenue. In that respect, what a company does with its money is perhaps the truest expression of its identity.

Numbers don't lie. As a company spends, it defines its identity and its culture. And so, it becomes quite simple to know how serious a firm is about participating in the Elevated Economy from the way it allocates its resources. If two people doing the same job receive different compensation, that is an issue.

Paying employees fairly shouldn't be controversial. It shouldn't have to be argued, but unfortunately, we still live in an age where the case must be made. It's been over 50 years since President John F. Kennedy signed the Equal Pay Act, so why is this still an issue? The career planning expert Dawn Rosenberg McKay says:

> Employers do not always abide by the Equal Pay Act of 1963 or by the other laws that require equal pay for equal work. In Fiscal Year 2006 (October 1, 2005 to September 30, 2006), the Equal Employment Opportunity Commission (EEOC) received 861

complaints about wage discrimination, which included accusations of employers violating the Equal Pay Act, Title VII of the
Civil Rights Act, the Age Discrimination in Employment Act
and the Americans With Disabilities Act (Charge Statistics: FY
1997 through FY 2006).[4]

A decade and a half following this study, things have not improved
much. According to workplace staffing and analysis firm Glassdoor:

> Today, the unadjusted pay gap between men and women in the
> US is 21.4 percent, meaning women earn, on average, $0.79 for
> every $1.00 men earn. This represents a 2.7 percentage point
> shrink in the unadjusted pay gap from three years ago, when
> women earned, on average, $0.76 for every $1.00 men earn.
>
> [However] 9 in 10 employees from around the globe believe
> men and women should be paid equally for equal work and
> experience.[5]

That last line is the most important for students of the Elevated
Economy. There is a massive gap between the realities of what businesses are doing and what consumers would like to see. A full 90
percent of the world wants men and women to be paid equally, and
yet the disparities remain.

The conscious consumer demand for pay equality in the Elevated
Economy is real, it's here, and the data is more transparent than ever.
Consumers and current and potential employees have more access to

---

4   https://www.thebalancecareers.com/why-equal-pay-for-women-would-benefit-the-u-s-
    economy-3514892.

5   https://www.glassdoor.com/employers/blog/eliminate-gender-pay-gap/.

data now than ever before, and are making decisions based on how firms behave.

CORNERSTONE THREE: IMPACT

One of the most successful early adopters of the Elevated Economy is Wells Fargo. Recently buffeted by a series of negative crises, its positive work goes largely unnoticed. Although you rarely hear the positive news from this firm, it is consistently participating in some of the most ambitious and effective corporate social responsibility (CSR) initiatives in the United States. This is not the type of company that spends one dollar helping others and $1 million telling the world about it either.

One of the reasons that Wells Fargo is able to do so much dramatic good in the world while keeping such an unusually low profile is because it focuses on creating practical good in practical spaces. What this means is that Wells Fargo prioritizes creating and executing philanthropic programs that create real benefit for its employees and the communities it operates in, rather than simply funneling millions to a charity.

There is nothing inherently wrong with giving to large or well-known charities; however, focusing locally enhances a firm's ability to be recognized by its employees, stakeholders, vendors, and suppliers. Wells Fargo's philanthropic housing and development programs turn its major corporate hubs into areas of civic and community recognition, which in turn improves employee engagement, retention, and recruitment, not to mention the goodwill generated among its customers.

Wells Fargo pours money into affordable housing, sustainable transportation, and local initiatives that matter most to the people in their area. They figured out that if you benefit the communities in which your company operates, you will also be benefiting your customers, civic leaders, employees, and their families. According to Wells Fargo: "We are proud of our legacy of serving and supporting those in need throughout the United States. We use our resources and expertise to address complex societal issues and pave a path to stability and financial success for the underserved."[6]

Its initiatives include intentional strategies to support family housing, financial education, disaster relief, military families and veterans, and the environment. It also has an extensive grant program for local charities and communities. All culminating in the fact that:

> In 2019, for the 10th year in a row, United Way Worldwide has recognized Wells Fargo as No. 1 in workplace giving. This distinction comes from thousands of team members who collectively pledged $75.3 million throughout 2018 and during Wells Fargo's companywide Community Support Campaign, which aims to lift communities and direct resources to pressing community challenges like education, hunger, homelessness, and more.[7]

Elevated companies need to put people over profits, or prioritize what I call interpersonal impact. It is no longer enough to include a blurb about a multi-million-dollar Red Cross donation. Elevated

---

6   https://www.wellsfargo.com/about/corporate-responsibility/community-giving/.

7   https://stories.wf.com/year-giving-wells-fargo-donates-444m-nearly-11000-nonprofits-2018/.

consumers want to see and feel the real impacts from the companies they work for, buy from, or engage with.

Engaging in interpersonal impact well can have myriad positive effects on a business's bottom line, and one of the best ways to measure this consistently is through employee retention. When companies are good citizens, they reap the rewards from the new consumers who consistently search for the signs of an elevated business before they buy.

The impact of this was on full display when Wells Fargo allowed a disastrous breach of trust to happen under its watch. In 2016, it was discovered that Wells Fargo employees had created over 2.1 million fake accounts in an attempt by some dishonest salespeople to boost their performance statistics. The news was met with shock and outrage and yet, somewhat surprisingly, the executive team's response was to shift more focus toward their employees instead of less. In 2017, Wells Fargo's former CEO Tim Sloan announced that he was determined to put his employees' needs above the needs of just about anything else, including profits. In a story related to the scandal, Reuters reported that:

> Wells Fargo stopped paying branch workers based on how many products they sold and increased its minimum pay rate to between $13.50 and $17 per hour, depending upon the market in which they work.
>
> "Turnover now in our retail bank is the lowest it's been, that I can recall, in my 30 years at the company," Sloan said at the Milken Institute Global Conference in Beverly Hills, California.[8]

---

8 https://www.reuters.com/article/us-milken-conference-wells-fargo-idUSKBN17X2BH.

Sloan, who got a battlefield promotion to the top job in October after his predecessor, John Stumpf, resigned under fire, said the bank has not had trouble attracting new employees since it changed its policies.

"When you put your shareholders first—I hope Warren Buffett isn't listening, by the way—but when you put them first, then you're going to make mistakes. Because you're going to make short-term decisions that aren't focused on creating a long-term, successful company," Sloan said.

This is the Elevated Economy in action. Firms are realizing that solely generating shareholder value doesn't generate much value for the company itself. But those that focus on improving their communities, their supply chains, and the lives of the employees they provide for are generating shareholder value while also simultaneously building more valuable organizations altogether.

CORNERSTONE FOUR: BRING THE MARKET

A "go-to-market" strategy is the plan for how a firm brings a product to market. GTM strategies include plans that identify the target audience, detail a marketing and advertising plan, and provide strategies for sales, distribution, and an evaluation of competition. Having a solid GTM strategy is tried and true business practice. But, like everything else in the Elevated Economy, even this has started to change.

The main idea behind a GTM plan is to use the firm's resources and sales to deliver its unique value proposition to customers. The result of this is a competitive advantage—and profits. We have a product or service at point A and the market is at point B. If we want to be successful, we must get our product or service all the way to point B—while making all the correct moves and avoiding the pitfalls along the way. If the team is successful, consumers make a purchase.

This model has a lot in common with pre-elevated business practices. In the old world, the product or service is king. The company's job is to make products or services and then call the market's attention to them. In the Elevated Economy, this is still the name of the game, but the focus has shifted to include the company itself.

Just like that sushi restaurant my friend saw—the one that championed its environmentally friendly status while saying nothing about the taste or quality of the food—in the Elevated Economy it is far less important to bring your product or service to a consumer than it is to bring that consumer to you. Whether it's something as blatant as that sushi restaurant, or more subtle signals from fast-food chains switching to plant-based alternatives, the go-to-market game has changed significantly and will continue to rapidly evolve.

A unique example of this can be seen in the video game industry. A recent trend in video games has been the inclusion of "loot boxes"—digital crates that contain mystery bonuses for players. These boxes cost small amounts of real cash for the chance to earn digital goods. The gambling aspects of the system have raised eyebrows from the PTA all the way to Congress. Legality aside, these loot boxes drew scorn from players around the world and were largely seen as predatory by the gaming community. The rub, however, is that these boxes generate millions upon millions of dollars for the studios and publishers.

In the old-world product-driven model this would simply be seen as an annoyance but not as a fundamental issue. Clearly the product fits with the market. Money is being made, and until a law is passed it will remain on the balance sheet for many fiscal years to come. But this is not how the world works anymore.

Electronic Arts (EA), one of the largest video game companies on earth, was the primary loot box offender of 2018. And then, just one year later, company executives took to trade shows, press releases, and unending Twitter barrages to point out how their new games have done away with this highly lucrative but frowned-upon practice. Now, loot boxes have become synonymous with corporate greed, and so gaming companies are abandoning them left and right—leaving millions on the table in the process.

In the Elevated Economy, firms are subtly replacing their GTM strategies with what I call "BTM" strategies. GTM stands for "go to market," but BTM stands for "bring the market." While GTM strategies attempt to get products or services to market, BTM strategies attempt to bring the market to them.

The goal of a GTM is to make sure a product fits with the market. The goal of a BTM, however, is to make sure that the market connects with the product and—more importantly—that the market connects with the company itself.

Disney+ was a BTM strategy in action. Rather than simply working harder to force bigger films and more expensive ticket prices down the market's throat at point B, Disney decided to build a system that would bring the market all the way back to meet it at point A. And they aren't the only ones taking advantage of this new way of thinking.

An example of this comes from my friend Christina Stembel, CEO of Farmgirl Flowers. This rapidly growing online florist delivers flowers all over the United States every day. The company describes itself online by saying:

> Our goal is to provide the best flowers and customer experience every single time. We promise to do what's right, and to do our very best, in everything we do. We're proud to design each bouquet by hand and with heart, source our flowers from farms that live up to our high ethical standards, and to create

good jobs. We're committed to living our values, and to do our very best for our customers, team, vendors, and environment.[9]

Ninety percent of that paragraph has nothing to do with flowers. The new brands of today are being built on values, not value. And the elevated consumers of today and tomorrow are rewarding them handsomely. So much so, that even titans like Disney and Electronic Arts would rather pivot from, or abandon, lucrative revenue streams to win hearts and minds as well as wallets. Not because they're nice. But because they want to be sustainable—to thrive for years to come. The old adage may be "The customer is always right." But in the Elevated Economy, that phrase could be extended with a few more words.

The customer is always right . . . or else.

Diversity and inclusion, pay equality, environmental and societal impacts, and Bring the Market strategy are the cornerstones that can help form the foundation of an elevated company. One fantastic example of a corporate leader doing this well is Bianca Gates, the CEO and co-founder of Birdies—a red-hot apparel startup that makes comfortable, stylish footwear. Bianca is able to lead a purpose-driven company built on these cornerstones because of a decision she made to live her own life in the exact same way. In a recent interview, she told me her story:

> I think as a young person graduating college, the idea of getting a job is, you need to make money, and ideally you want to work for a company that resonates with you, so in my early 20s working for Viacom selling TV shows to advertisers resonated with me. But I think as you get further into your career, you ask yourself deeper, more thoughtful questions about my meaning

9 https://farmgirlflowers.com/the-farmgirl-way.

and my purpose in life and what am I getting up for every single day. And for me, it was when I had my daughter Sofia, who's now 10, when I started to really ask myself this question. I'm selling reality TV programming to advertisers, and there was just no meaning and no purpose.

And now, as a mother, I feel like I was destined to do something bigger, and have a bigger impact on the world, and I wasn't finding that I was getting that through my job. It was very much focused on my W2 and me, and enjoying what I did—but beyond that, it just felt very soulless. Then I read Sheryl Sandberg's commencement speech at Barnard College, and [Sandberg] talked about leaning in and finding a purpose—just really, "What is the motivating force behind what you do every day?" And I just remember thinking, "I'm not motivated beyond making money, and so what am I going to do beyond that."

And so, when I read her commencement speech, I thought, Facebook was a mission-driven company, and it was the first time that I had thought about mission-driven anything. And their mission was very simple, it was to make the world more open and connected, and being the daughter of immigrant parents from Latin America, connecting with my relatives in Latin America for free using this platform was everything for me. And if we could help everybody else around the world connect with their family members and start businesses using this platform, that is something I can rally behind, and that meant more to me than my W2. In fact, funny story is when I got the offer to work at Facebook, the offer was making 100,000 dollars a year less, and it was a three-hour-a-day commute there and back, versus my 20-minute commute that I had at Viacom. I took the job anyway because I was so desperate for a mission and a greater purpose in life . . . I did that for six years. I did that commute for an hour and a half there and an hour and a half back, and I had a two-year-old and then, shortly after starting, I got pregnant with my second child, and I was sick with morning sickness. . . . And yet with the learning curve and the commute and the much lower salary, I came home every day skipping—I felt invigorated. And so, it was at that point where I thought, "For the rest of my life, every decision I make in terms of what I do with my day has to have a purpose and a meaning behind it, including work."[10]

Birdies is still young, but it is already generating millions in revenue per year. And it's doing so with sustainable materials, proactive hiring practices, and a keen eye on its impact on society. It's a fantastic example of how business is being done well and what behaviors customers are prepared to reward in the coming decades.

Purpose is a quantifiable metric. Glassdoor, one of the world's largest job and recruiting sites, released a survey conducted by The Harris Poll measuring sentiment around mission and culture in the workplace today, along with the level of importance of both. The survey uncovers the importance of culture and company mission to recruitment and retention, as well as the extent to which job seekers are now looking for employers whose values align with their own personal values.

"Having a compelling mission, culture, and values are critical when it comes to attracting and retaining top talent in a competitive job market—it is what differentiates each and every employer," said

---

10 Gates, discussion with author.

Christian Sutherland-Wong, Glassdoor president and chief operating officer. "It's clear that job seekers are seeking more meaningful workplace experiences. Job seekers want to be paid fairly, but they too want to work for a company whose values align with their own and whose mission they can fully get behind."[11]

---

11   https://theharrispoll.com/culture-over-cash-glassdoor-multi-country-survey-finds-more-than-half-of-employees-prioritize-workplace-culture-over-salary/.

CHAPTER 7

ESG

"You will not be remembered for what you have done,
but rather for what you do next."

—Professor Robert S. Kaplan, Harvard Business School

I started my first business in 2000 as a sole proprietor. Being on my own gave me immense freedom to establish the corporate culture I wanted. Although, I admit, the office happy hours were a little lonely.

Soon enough, though, my fledgling dreams began to take flight. Suddenly, I was incorporated. I had employees. And then more employees. And then even more employees. Recognizing the demand for digital media—and experts who could create and manage it—the company became so large it needed to move to a bigger building. A building with its own zip code: 10118, to be exact. The Empire State Building.

Growing up, I was fascinated with New York City. My parents had a framed picture of the Manhattan skyline on our wall. As a kid,

I would stare at it for hours, imagining all the people in all of those buildings—it seemed otherworldly to me, impossible and incredible that that world existed. And so, owning a business headquartered in the Empire State Building felt like the culmination of a lifelong dream. But I quickly realized that maintaining this incredible new reality was going to be complicated.

At first, meetings consisted of me, myself, and I. Decisions were made quickly. Alignment was a breeze. And since I wasn't about to quit, employee retention was flying high at 100 percent. As more people joined, however, leading my firm and providing for the livelihood of my employees meant making decisions, decisions that reflected the best interests of more than just myself. To make those decisions, I needed strong values. Fortunately for me, I had plenty of time to figure out who we wanted to be by the time I made it to the Empire State Building.

I thought about what we would do as a business, but I also thought about what we wouldn't do. Both are important drivers of culture. I knew what we would focus on, what we would say "yes" to, and I knew what we'd say "no" to—we would never, under any circumstances, take on clients that made their income from tobacco, gambling, or pornography. This was a hard line for me. Even before the rise of ESG and SRI made it appealing to start a company based on values, I was determined not to lose my soul in the big city. But the city wasn't going to make it easy.

A few years into operating the business with even more employees, we got an opportunity. The startups I advise these days might even call it "the" opportunity. A contract was on the table for more money than I'd ever seen. This contract would have cemented our financial future for the next year. It would have provided enough revenue to nearly double the size of my company overnight. But there was a problem.

The client was R. J. Reynolds Tobacco Company, specifically

American Spirit—one of their most successful cigarette brands. They were finally ready to take the digital leap, and heard we were the firm to talk to. Their offer was enormous. Surely taking this contract was worth putting a few scratches on my own sense of morality, right? Surely the best way to fund my dreams and provide for my employees was to take the deal, right? How could I live with myself if I said no and we hit a rough financial quarter? How could I tell one of my employees I would have to let her go because I wasn't willing to help sell a few cigarettes?

But then, as corny as this might sound, I thought about my kids—the kids I didn't even have yet. Did I want them to see this company's logo on their dad's company's website? Did I want them to read a testimonial from the CEO of a tobacco company praising their dad for putting more cigarettes into the world? Did I want to take them on vacation, knowing that R. J. Reynolds Tobacco had essentially paid for it?

The situation was complicated, but the answer to those questions wasn't. I did not want that legacy for my children, and I didn't want it for my employees, or for their children either.

We rejected the contract, and all of the money, security, and prosperity it had to offer. And as soon as we did, those guidelines of yeses and nos became something much bigger than a reflection of my own youthful ideals. They became the backbone of the culture of my company. And that culture became just as important as our products and services.

By the time I sold the company, our employee retention rate was five times the industry average. It was extremely rare for one of our employees to leave us. There are many reasons that this was true. But I think one of the biggest was that they believed in our culture, and they wanted to do well by doing good. In short, they didn't want R. J. Reynolds Tobacco Company taking their kids on vacation either.

Fast-forward to today and this story is more relevant than it has ever been. Right now, every indicator is telling us that when corporate values change in favor of better environmental, social, and governance practices, employees stay longer, market share increases, and profits rise for those businesses.

There wasn't a word for it yet, but my refusal to work with R. J. Reynolds Tobacco Company's American Spirit brand was my first experience in building and running what today's economists would call an ESG company, one focused on elevated environmental, social, and governance practices. That lesson is important because underneath all of the statistics, predictions, and best practices that follow, being an ESG firm really boils down to one simple idea: that stakeholders are ready and willing to reward firms that put values first.

This change has created a massive wave of opportunity. And not just the opportunity to build better businesses, but to build a better world. Because, at the end of the day, we all want to take our kids on a vacation we can be proud of.

WHERE WE CAME FROM: THE PATH TO THE TRIPLE BOTTOM LINE

ESG is having a moment in the global economy. However, despite its prevalence, ESG is not synonymous with an Elevated Economy. An Elevated Economy is one potential outcome of the sudden rise in ESG. ESG serves as an important yardstick, and understanding it is vital to understanding the epoch of elevated economics we are entering.

It's important to note that although we currently use the term ESG to describe them, ethically minded corporations are not new. All business school students can recount the case study on the Tylenol recall.

In 1982, cyanide-laced pills were found in several bottles of Tylenol and seven people died. The leadership of Johnson & Johnson (J&J) had a choice. They could take all the stock off the shelves, take the loss (estimated to be well over $100 million), open the door for competitors to decimate its market share, and risk permanently damaging the Tylenol brand. Or they could decide to not take action, and hope it didn't happen again.

Even in the face of those deaths, business pundits at the time were still shocked to see J&J make the hard choice. They pulled all of the stock off the shelves of every store. They lost market share. But they did not damage their brand. Instead, Tylenol and J&J became synonymous with integrity. Here was a company that would spare no expense to fix its mistakes and ensure they never happen again. Decades later, Tylenol remains the leading over-the-counter pain reliever in the United States.

Johnson and Johnson was an ESG company before the term existed. Today, this commitment to values remains the cornerstone of their business. You can still read the credo the company adopted in 1943. They followed their credo before the Tylenol recall, during it, and they follow it today. In it, they name four stakeholders: the medical professionals they serve (the customers), the employees who work for them, the communities in which they do business, and lastly, the shareholders. In fact, the credo says of shareholders:

> Our final responsibility is to our stockholders. Business must make a sound profit. We must experiment with new ideas. Research must be carried on, innovative programs developed, investments made for the future and mistakes paid for. New equipment must be purchased, new facilities provided, and new products launched. Reserves must be created to provide for adverse times. When we operate according to these principles, the stockholders should realize a fair return.

Recently, a council of CEOs featuring the likes of Amazon's Jeff Bezos made headlines for declaring a new business paradigm that puts shareholder value at the bottom and ESG concepts like health, wellness, and environmentalism at the top. Their declaration hit the world like a freight train, but, as evidenced by J&J, these ideas have been around for a long time.

What's changed is that embracing those ideas is no longer the secret deliberation of corporations like J&J. Embracing those ideas is now a transparent, fundamental principle of businesses, both large and small.

In the book *Problem Solving: HBS Alumni Making a Difference in the World*, coauthor Howard Stevenson alludes to a much longer history of ESG and "ethical" investing. In an interview, the professor was asked if his readers would be surprised to find out that corporations solving social problems is nothing new. He responds by saying:

> The discussion about the role of business in society and the responsibilities of business leaders has been going on since Scottish economist Adam Smith wrote *The Wealth of Nations* in 1776. CSR [corporate social responsibility] is a relatively new movement espousing a triple bottom line of people, planet, and profits, rather than a single-minded focus on shareholder value. People of my vintage recall when business leadership was about serving customers at a profit and giving back to your community was expected. And many of today's business students arrive with a commitment to social impact through or alongside their professional careers.[1]

And so, while the philosophy and principles behind sustainable investing—and the way businesses are behaving to receive that

---

1 https://hbswk.hbs.edu/item/these-entrepreneurs-take-a-pragmatic-approach-to-solving-social-problems.

investment—are nothing new, the era in which they begin to move from theory to fringe to fact is beginning to dawn. The triple bottom line alluded to by Stevenson is on track to one day be just as ubiquitous in business school curricula as the single bottom line is today.

During my time at Harvard Business School, we often heard the school referred to as the "West Point of Capitalism." At the time we laughed, but the metaphor holds up. Most business education pushes toward one single goal: maximize shareholder value. The goal is to win, and the terms used in business school are mostly military metaphors: we were taught to "capture" market share; we referred to customers or companies we might buy as "targets"; we talked about our "front line" employees who are "in the field"; and of course, we "execute." To see that this winner-take-all, us-versus-them definition of business leadership is beginning to fade speaks volumes about how powerful this change is. We are moving from a single-bottom-line mindset to a triple-bottom-line mindset that includes not just shareholders, but all stakeholders. According to *The Economist*,

> The phrase "the triple bottom line" was first coined in 1994 by John Elkington, the founder of a British consultancy called SustainAbility. His argument was that companies should be preparing three different (and quite separate) bottom lines. One is the traditional measure of corporate profit—the "bottom line" of the profit and loss account. The second is the bottom line of a company's "people account"—a measure in some shape or form of how socially responsible an organisation has been throughout its operations. The third is the bottom line of the company's "planet" account—a measure of how environmentally responsible it has been. The triple bottom line (TBL) thus consists of three Ps: profit, people, and planet. It aims to measure the financial, social and environmental performance of the corporation

over a period of time. Only a company that produces a TBL is taking account of the full cost involved in doing business.[2]

This triple bottom line is reflected by its similarly triplicate initialism: E, S, and G. Modern businesses are flouting the cutthroat ambitions of the past, and instead, more and more are choosing to protect the environment; to pursue improvements for their employees, vendors, and customers; to initiate internal governance; and—ultimately—to change the definition of the bottom line from solely profit to doing well by being good.

So now the question becomes: If this trend is indeed so powerful, just how well are its early adopters performing?

WHERE WE ARE NOW: WATER-BOTTLE SHOES

Forbes recently splashed this headline across its homepage: "The Power of Purpose: How Adidas Will Make $1 Billion Helping Solve the Problem of Ocean Plastic.*"

The article delved into Adidas's recent announcement that it would be doing a collaboration with Parley for the Oceans—a nonprofit committed to reducing waste products in natural water sources. The partnership would see Adidas releasing a limited-edition sports shoe made entirely from recycled plastics pulled directly from contaminated oceans. Each of the 7,000 shoes in the initial run would be created from roughly 11 plastic water bottles. Adidas said it plans to expand this eco-friendly technology into both its mainstream shoe and apparel lines.

This is good news for the planet, but it is fascinating news for business leaders. Because while most articles surrounding this news were praising the brand's good environmental citizenship, a *Forbes* article

---

2 https://www.economist.com/news/2009/11/17/triple-bottom-line.

decided to focus on the massive windfall that Adidas was projected to receive as a result of this "charity." According to the article:

> Adidas has announced it intends to sell five million pairs of ocean plastic shoes—at an average retail price of around $220. This means the brand is set to make more than a billion dollars in revenue by trying to solve one of the world's biggest environmental problems. Adidas also announced that it intends to use 100% recycled polyester in all of its products (where solutions exist) by 2024 (Adidas makes 403 million pairs of shoes annually).[3]

Moves like this used to be labeled as "stunts" or "marketing," but in the age of the Elevated Economy, the Adidas strategy takes on much greater significance. This is not a one-time maneuver to score some political or cultural points. This is a massive top-to-bottom shake-up in supply chains, production, manufacturing, shipping, sales, and advertising. This one move may net the company $1 billion over time, but the cost to pivot toward that billion is significant. In days past, this would have been seen as a short-term cash grab or marketing ploy. But things are different now. Business is different.

These water-bottle shoes are more than a stunt. They are an early move in a very large game that Adidas and other global brands have all begun to play. Because the prize is too massive to ignore.

Another company, Imperfect Foods, has made "waste" its product. According to its website, 40 percent of food produced in the United States goes uneaten; $218 billion of food is thrown away every year; 21 percent of our water supply is used to produce wasted food each

---

3   https://www.forbes.com/sites/afdhelaziz/2018/10/29/the-power-of-purpose-how-adidas-will-make-1-billion-helping-solve-the-problem-of-ocean-plastic/#5935111ed215.

year; and 20 billion pounds of fresh produce go unharvested or unsold every year. This isn't because this food is inedible, rotten, or poisoned. It's because it isn't perfect.

Supermarkets want unblemished, beautifully colored, and uniformly sized fruits and vegetables. A misshapen apple, a scarred potato, an extra-small egg—these are deemed unsalable to the conglomerate grocery stores, so they are discarded. Some go to make juices or canned foods or other products, but the preceding numbers and percentages reflect what doesn't.

Enter Imperfect Foods, whose motto is "Groceries on a Mission," and whose mantra is "If food can be saved, then we will save it." Other pertinent phrases include "Good for you and yours. Good for the planet." These groceries also cost 30 percent less than grocery store produce and they lack neither nutrition nor freshness. They simply lack beauty. There are other kinds of discarded food products included in Imperfect Foods as well—surplus, results of changing customer demand, repackaging, and so on, but the Imperfect label covers them all.

If ESG is a measurement of how individual firms are measured against environmental, social, and governance practices, then SRI (socially responsible investing) measures how much money investors decide to invest in those firms. The numbers are astounding, and Adidas is playing the long game. According to CNBC:

> There is now more than $12 trillion invested in a variety of socially responsible ways. That's 1 out of 4 of the total assets under management in the US alone.
>
> SRI assets are growing at nearly 40% year-over-year since 2016, according to the US SIF Foundation's "Report on US Sustainable, Responsible and Impact Investing Trends."[4]

---

4   https://www.cnbc.com/2019/05/06/socially-responsible-investing-is-hot-with-no-signs-of-cooling-off.html.

However, the response from firms to this explosion of activity is lagging, not leading. According to the same report:

> Nearly every S&P 500 firm now issues a sustainability report. Yet businesses are not celebrating their social impact—even though many have embraced corporate social responsibility practices.[5]

ESG can be tightly correlated and linked with socially responsible investing. If somebody is choosing to invest in a company, they might look at its ESG practices, its ESG score, and so on. On the investing side, it's becoming much more commonplace for someone to ask a wealth manager to put an ESG screen across all of their investments.

More and more people are now saying, "Hey, look, I'm happy to invest in the market, but just no guns." Or, "I'm happy to invest in the market, but just no extraction companies like oil or gas." In Economics 101 we would call this a change in demand. And when demand changes, supply necessarily must change as well. And "supply" in this case means the public company's actions, as measured by its ESG score.

In a recent Stanford study, it was determined that companies with high ESG scores from trusted third parties are typically correlated to overall higher profitability and stock value. The conclusion of the study—which examined 55 separate reports on ESG corporations—is that companies committed to ESG perform better and have lower risk; however, their socially conscious actions are largely being priced into securities markets.

This research shows that companies committed to environmental and social goals have better performance and lower risk. However, the important thing for change agents to be aware of is that this relationship is still considered "modest," as the market and analysts continue to grapple with issues of causality and correlation.

---

5 Ibid.

Does a commitment to environmental or social goals make companies more profitable, or are more profitable companies able to spend more on these activities?

The basic premise of the Elevated Economy is that a change in demand—driven by a new consumer ethic—does in fact support the premise that a commitment to environmental and social goals makes companies more profitable. For the first time in the history of capitalism, the numbers are reporting what optimistic economists have always hoped: that the arc of consumer behavior ultimately bends toward the just.

The issue, however, is not proving to corporate change makers that this is happening—data is, by nature, open to interpretation. Rather, the issue is getting them to believe it and take action based on that belief. The shift from brutalism to altruism in the world's economic system is just around the corner. The red line is approaching. Or, recall as the Nielsen report put it:

> Corporate responsibility and sustainability strategies may take different shapes around the world, but one thing is clear: consumers are using their spending power to effect the change they want to see. This isn't a trend a company can simply sidestep. Sooner or later, whether through government regulation, sheer force of nature, or public outcry, companies will need to respond. No matter what market you're in, connecting sustainability factors to how it impacts consumers is the key.[6]

In the tech industry, there's a concept known as a singularity. A singularity is a moment of technological change that makes the

---

6　https://www.nielsen.com/us/en/insights/report/2018/finding-success-through-sustainability/

society before the change unfathomable to society after the change. The Internet was a singularity. So was the telephone. And so is this.

Even the NASDAQ itself sees that the writing is on the wall. In its recently published environmental, social, and governance guide, the minds behind one of the largest barometers of market performance had this to say about the rise of ESG and its effect on consumer behavior and corporate prosperity:

> While ESG factors are at times called non-financial, how a company manages them undoubtedly has financial consequences. The very term non-financial is a controversial point of reference, because many believe that ESG information is no less relevant or useful to an investor in assessing the financial prospects and operational performance of a company than information channeled through traditional accounting practices.
>
> A range of studies have found correlation between companies with good ESG practices and a lower cost of capital, lower stock price volatility, and better valuation over the long term. Nasdaq is now persuaded that a correlative exists, and it seems to exert positive influence for listed companies.[7]

Business leaders like to think in numbers, but the bigger reality is that the hearts and minds of people are changing—and those hearts and minds are attached directly to their wallets.

The corporations that embrace this momentum toward ESG may become unrecognizable to those on the other side of the dawning economic singularity that is driving us toward the new Elevated Economy. They will be making decisions and employing strategies

---

7   https://www.nasdaq.com/ESG-Guide.

that their counterparts of yesteryear would call foolish at best and irresponsible at worst. As the economy elevates, ESG-friendly companies will be on the winning side of that singularity. But the rest won't just become unrecognizable.

They will become extinct.

HOW GOOD IS GOOD ENOUGH?

Numbers and sentiments are powerful, but they are only as valuable as their ability to reflect our reality. It's all well and good to say that "good" companies will see higher profits and increased market capitalization, but does that actually manifest itself in the real world?

I live in a part of the world that is ruled by big tech. I'm within 50 miles of global offices for Apple, Facebook, Google, Twitter, Tesla, Uber, Netflix, and many more. These firms present themselves as decent firms, doing good in the world, yet Facebook consistently fumbles the private data of its users. Google and Apple seem not only interested but eager to censor themselves in order to gain access to China's billion-person customer market despite that nation's repeated human rights violations. Amazon uses people like machines to fulfill online orders in 24 hours or less.

However, despite all this, these companies aren't just successful, they are the most successful corporations in history. The Elevated Economy demands ethical corporations, and yet our current landscape seems ruled by titans that can be, at times, perceived as anything but. If the Elevated Economy is really approaching, shouldn't these companies be shrinking, struggling, and failing consistently? The answer is: no. They aren't going to fail. They are going to change. And it's already begun.

A professor of mine used to say that it is "better to be at the table than on the menu," and when it comes to the FAANGs (Facebook, Amazon, Apple, Netflix, and Google) and their fellow juggernauts, this concept is being proved as the economy introduces a new set of best practices. The true test of our economy's current state is not to measure how many of the old guard are failing. It's to measure how many of them are changing.

Take Google and China, for example. For Google to get into China and compete with Baidu, which censors Internet content in lockstep with the communist government, it has to significantly censor its most popular product: search. Doing so means giving in to an inhumane, totalitarian Communist regime. However, not doing so means getting up and leaving the table altogether. Refusing to censor, and to therefore not enter China, doesn't make Google noble. It makes them politically and economically obsolete. Google's absence in China does not lead to a more free and open state. It leads to Baidu.

Being a change agent in the Elevated Economy doesn't require a company to be perfect. It requires them to be trying. This isn't an excuse for companies that are slow on the uptake. Hesitance will breed the same result as inaction: the death of the firm as consumer attitudes remove it from consideration. But right now, seeing companies with unethical behavior does not disprove the importance of embracing the Elevated Economy. Because everywhere you look, companies aren't just moving toward ESG. They are sprinting.

BEYOND ESG

The ultimate culmination of the growing focus on ESG goes far beyond the facts and figures of today. The fact that McDonald's is preparing meatless options and Amazon is rewriting its warehouse policies is just the tip of a very large iceberg. The true resonance of the Elevated Economy is only just beginning to be heard. It will come to fruition—as all economic matters do—in time, as we move from one generation to the next.

I'm an investor. And I like to think I'm a pretty informed and careful one. I've moved assets into ESG-focused funds, and whereas I know I'm not the first person to do that, I certainly won't be the last. Investing is binary—when money moves into one account, it leaves another. And when money moves, so do businesses.

Generation Z will be a big driver of change. The money that they move will have consequences. This generation of ecologically minded investors will not support fossil fuel companies that contribute to toxic air quality and climate change. They will refuse to live in fear of being murdered in their schools because legislators are too gutless to pass meaningful gun laws. They aren't interested in filling their lungs with death from the tobacco companies or buying from companies that aren't taking steps to combat racism. They have opinions and values that reflect the new paradigm they bring with them to adulthood. And once they get there, they won't just have values. They will have money to express those values at scale. And they are only the beginning.

Today the changes we are seeing in socially responsible investing, purchase decisions, and ESG may be incremental. But tomorrow they won't be. Tomorrow those changes will have evolved to be the immutable reality of a brand-new customer base. Economists are trained to think long term. The business leaders of today are welcome to test the consumers of tomorrow. But as giants like the FAANGs continue to change—albeit incrementally—it seems clear that the smart money would stay at the table instead of choosing to place themselves on the menu.

In his interview with Dina Gerdeman, Professor Stevenson of HBS posited:

> There was a sense that ethics were forgotten as investor capital-
> ism became the new business model, with shareholder value and

personal gain at its core. It sparked considerable soul searching at business schools and discussion of whether and how ethics can be taught.

Many schools have made programmatic and other changes geared to heightening students' awareness of corporate and personal accountability. At HBS, I actually think that—as with many developments—it is the students who are driving ethics back to the forefront again. I think they are saying "No, that's not what leadership is about, and that's not what I want to be."[8]

The West Point of Capitalism is changing its marching orders because its "soldiers" are demanding it. That is beyond insubordination. It's a downright coup. And, as Stevenson points out, it's working. Just down the river from the HBS campus, professors are singing the same tune. In my interview with MIT professor Scott Stern, he stated simply that "we have to figure out how to make companies accountable.[9]

• • •

Years after I refused that tobacco company contract, I knew I had made the right decision. I had had the extreme pleasure and good fortune of working with some of the most dedicated and hardworking people anyone could ever hope to employ, the company had grown and then been acquired, and I was enjoying a happy new career investing and advising companies big and small. I wondered what would have happened if I had taken the money from the American Spirit

8 https://hbswk.hbs.edu/item/these-entrepreneurs-take-a-pragmatic-approach-to-solving-social-problems.

9 Scott Stern, MIT professor, in discussion with the author, April 2020.

cigarette brand and all the opportunity that would have come with it. It might have yielded some immediate results. But I know they wouldn't have been as spectacular as what came next.

What if?

Years after that decision, a relatively small company caught my eye. It had nothing to do with tech at all. It was a racing and leadership company whose founder rows across oceans for a living. As I researched my potential investment, this small company began to represent for me the true ideals behind the Elevated Economy: adventure, integrity, and possibility.

What if our economy was not based on increasing value for hordes of nameless shareholders at any cost to society or the planet? What if customers realized that businesses need them? What if businesses only did well when they did good?

What if?

Today I am an investor in that racing and leadership company. There are many things I love about it and what it represents, but perhaps my favorite thing is the name of the boat that the team rowed across the Atlantic Ocean to capture the world record. I see that boat, and its ability to conquer the ocean, like humanity and its ability to conquer its own base instincts in pursuit of a better world.

And its name: *The American Spirit.*

CHAPTER 8

LIKE SALES IN AN HOURGLASS

"Nothing in this world can take the place of persistence. Talent will not; nothing is more common than unsuccessful men with talent. Genius will not; unrewarded genius is almost a proverb. Education will not; the world is full of educated derelicts. Persistence and determination alone are omnipotent. The slogan Press On! has solved and always will solve the problems of the human race."

—Calvin Coolidge

"Brand loyalty" was the exciting new buzzword of postwar marketing teams. Back when the Baby Boomers were still babies, their parents were enjoying an explosion of cheap housing, good jobs, and disposable income. This upheaval was similar in scale to the Elevated Economy today; a sudden change in consumer behavior was driving a significant course correction for most major corporations. The race was on to capture the pocketbooks of returning soldiers and their families. In light of increased competition, a new tactic was developed. And soon brands were selling something above and beyond their core products or services. They called it: "lifestyle."

An article in *The Atlantic*, "How Brands Were Born: A Brief History of Modern Marketing," crystallizes the point where this change occurred. An exploding population and skyrocketing average income created a groundswell of potential for corporations both new and old. According to the article:

> The shift from simple products to brands has not been sudden or inevitable. You could argue that it grew out of the standardization of quality products for consumers in the middle of the 20th century, which required companies to find a new way to differentiate themselves from their competitors.
>
> In the 1950s, consumer packaged goods companies like Procter and Gamble, General Foods and Unilever developed the discipline of brand management, or marketing as we know it today, when they noticed the quality levels of products being offered by competitors around them improve. A brand manager would be responsible for giving a product an identity that distinguishes it from nearly indistinguishable competitors.
>
> This required an understanding of the target consumer and what we call a "branded proposition" that offered not only functional but also emotional value. Over time, the emotional value would create a buffer against functional parity. As long as the brand was perceived to offer superior value to its competitors, the company offering the brand could charge a little more for its products. If this brand "bonus" was bigger than the cost of building a brand (the additional staff and often advertising costs), the company came out ahead.[1]

---

1 https://www.theatlantic.com/business/archive/2011/10/how-brands-were-born-a-brief-history-of-modern-marketing/246012/.

Two of these core concepts, the Branded Proposition and the power of emotional attachments on buying decisions, are as relevant and vital for understanding what's happening now in the Elevated Economy as they were in the 1950s to understand what was happening then with the postwar boom. Firms today are in the midst of redefining what their branded propositions should be, as the importance of their ability to generate strong emotional resonance increases. Fifty years ago, capturing customer emotion was the key to standing out in a crowded marketplace; but from today onward, emotion is what ensures a brand's ability to stay relevant in the Elevated Economy.

Today's marketing and product development operations are still very much focused on creating interest in products or services that were designed to succeed at scale through rapid growth and unending expansion. But as consumer behavior changes, this race-to-the-finish mindset may not be what yields the best results.

A study from Nigeria's Olabisi Onabanjo University explains this potential misstep in greater detail. The authors theorize that:

> Marketers and organizational managers are interested in managing their organizations to achieve surplus (profit) which is often used as the greatest yardstick for organizational performance. Marketers in particular, in doing this, manipulate the marketing mix to stimulate exchange between the firm and customers. However, in recent times, increased attention has been paid to brand loyalty. Thus, this study was conducted to investigate the correlation between brand loyalty and organizational profitability.
>
> . . . The results show that organizational profitability is significantly and positively related to brand loyalty measures tested with R values of 0.749 significant 95% confidence level. Based

on these results, it was concluded that organizational profitability is a function of brand loyalty. This finding has implication for marketing managers and organizations in general in designing their various marketing strategies.[2]

The key takeaway is that firms that build, ship, and iterate primarily for profit are taking the less efficient path to profitability. But the firms that organize their efforts around creating brands that consumers will become loyal to, rather than products they want to buy, are seeing better results on the balance sheet. As Method Products CEO Drew Fraser put it:

> When our consumers get our products home, they realize it's a product that actually works. And this is a kind of backdoor loyalty. They may have bought the product because the packaging looks good, but they realize "it really cleans my clothes. It really cleans my counters." And then they [get to] know about our sustainable practices, they get to know that's a non-toxic formula. They get to know that the bottle is 100% PCR [post-consumer resin]. And so, we really kind of have that backdoor loyalty from our customers.
>
> . . . We were one of the original B Corp, certified companies, and it's something that we endorsed from the very beginning. During our last certification, we were ranked the fifth highest B Corp in the world—it was an amazing feat. It was one that carried across North America and Europe and beyond. And it's something that we're very proud of. So, given how rigorous the B Corp certification process is, and how it defines success,

whether it's traditional environmental and planet practices, to how you work with your team and your employees and the communities in which you do business, to have that type of score, that validation was quite gratifying.[3]

What began as a competitive advantage in the 1950s is rapidly becoming the most probable path to profitability for companies in the Elevated Economy. Corporate leaders need to strongly consider reorganizing their priorities if their primary goal is to reach the hearts and minds of those with the most economic agency.

This phenomenon isn't just economic, it's also biological. According to recent research, humans make buying decisions primarily with their hearts, not their minds. Antonio Damasio, professor of neuroscience at the University of Southern California, explains how modern brains respond to brands:

> It's been studied again and again; MRI tests have shown that when subjects evaluate products or brands, their limbic systems (where our feelings, memory, and value judgments originate) light up, while the data processing and analysis centers of their brains are left largely unstimulated. In other words, most of the purchase decisions people make are emotional, not practical.
>
> When the decisions humans make are largely based on how they feel, marketers can capitalize by communicating a feeling and removing emphasis on the cold hard facts. You need to appeal to the human, not the buyer.[4]

---

3 Fraser, discussion with author.

4 https://www.accounteer.com/blog/3-things-buyers-look-for-in-a-brand.

This has always been the ideal goal of sales and marketing teams—obsessed customers who evangelize their brand to others with the zeal of a born-again Christian. As the economy and its core customer base continue to evolve, fostering positive customer sentiment and loyalty is more important than ever. The best way to make sure your company is in a position to benefit from the coming revolution is to elevate every aspect of your business, including the products and services you provide.

Success in the Elevated Economy will be measured by your firm's ability to win the hearts and minds of its customers. What a product is has never been less important, and how a brand makes a person feel has never been more relevant. Products and services still have to be "good." The coffee still has to be hot, the shirt still has to fit, but emotion is even more important in Jeff Bezos's America than it was in Norman Rockwell's. Now as then, a strong positive emotional link can cover a multitude of setbacks and protect against the seductive advances of competitors.

In the Elevated Economy, you don't win by offering products and services people are willing to vote for with their dollars; you do it by offering products or services they *want* to vote for. The difference is subtle, but crossing that gap is the key to thriving in the economic world ahead.

THE NEW FUNNEL: THE BUYER BECOMES THE SELLER

The *Harvard Business Review* published an article with an opinion that strongly contradicts my own and that of researchers like Professor Damasio. The piece, titled "Customer Loyalty Is Overrated," uses the headline-stirring redesign of the Facebook-owned Instagram photo-sharing app's logo in late 2016. The app's icon was changed from a cartoonish image of an old-school, Kodak-style camera to a simple square overlaid on top of a hyper-modern purple and orange gradient.

The immediate response from Instagram's one-billion-plus users was almost universally negative. People didn't like the change, and the authors of this *HBR* article use this as evidence for their primary thesis: consumers don't buy based on ideals, they do so based on convenience and consistent positive experiences.

Essentially, the authors theorize that every buying decision becomes an automatic prioritization moment for the average consumer. As the article states:

> An assumption implicit in that definition is that consumers are making deliberate, perhaps even rational, decisions. Their reasons for buying products and services may be emotional, but they always result from somewhat conscious logic. Therefore, a good strategy figures out and responds to that logic.
>
> But the idea that purchase decisions arise from conscious choice flies in the face of much research in behavioral psychology. The brain, it turns out, is not so much an analytical machine as a gap-filling machine: It takes noisy, incomplete information from the world and quickly fills in the missing pieces on the basis of past experience. Intuition—thoughts,

opinions, and preferences that come to mind quickly and without reflection but are strong enough to act on—is the product of this process . . .

In short, research into the workings of the human brain suggests that the mind loves automaticity more than just about anything else—certainly more than engaging in conscious consideration. Given a choice, it would like to do the same things over and over again. If the mind develops a view over time that Tide gets clothes cleaner, and Tide is available and accessible on the store shelf or the web page, the easy, familiar thing to do is to buy Tide yet another time.[5]

This is an interesting counter-theory to my own, and I believe that exploring it can help drive home one of the key truths of the Elevated Economy: that the decision-making consumers of the next several decades will be making buying decisions primarily through an identity-driven, emotion-first, highly idealistic matrix. The authors of this article believe that a combination of recency and confirmation bias is what drives consumers to cash registers both now and in the immediate future. But following this thinking can prove downright dangerous to your firm, as it represents a fundamental and potentially fatal misunderstanding of just how significantly different the coming generation of consumers is from the current one.

In a recent column, *Marketing Land*'s Adam Grow—the former SVP for Global Commercial Operations at Rakuten—challenged the hierarchy of needs proposed in the *HBR* piece. New consumers, he argues, are not as primitive as some analysts may lead you to believe. He culminates his argument by laying out what he believes to be a

---

5   https://hbr.org/2017/01/customer-loyalty-is-overrated.

more accurate sketch of the decision-making framework being used by a new generation of consumers. He calls this the "Brand Affinity Hierarchy," and he explains it as such:

> There are striking similarities between the levels of Maslow's hierarchy and the way consumers shop for products. When we apply these theories to real consumer shopping behaviors, we get a hierarchy that includes various levels of brand affinity, such as awareness, infatuation, fidelity and evangelism.
>
> Consumers shopping for their basic needs simply need a product to do what it's meant to do. But as consumers move along the brand affinity hierarchy, their motivations expand and they begin to care about the benefits the product offers.
>
> This relationship further evolves as consumers develop trust in the brand, which can lead to infatuation. At this point, they feel that a specific brand contributes to their personal betterment, and they experience feelings of affection, appreciation, and even obsession.
>
> To achieve brand loyalty, a brand must facilitate consumers reaching their maximum potential. The brand must connect with the consumer's core values and reflect who they are—they simply can't live without the brand.[6]

Grow has data to back up his claims. While still at Rakuten, he worked with the company's research team to put numbers to the way consumers think. His results indicate a strong trend toward idealistic, emotion-heavy decision-making rather than the more primordial instincts suggested by the *HBR* article. According to Grow:

---

6   https://marketingland.com/makes-people-love-brands-love-208923.

As consumers move along the brand affinity hierarchy, they become more valuable to the brand, making more purchases, purchasing more frequently and spending more money.

. . . Our data shows that as consumers transition through the various levels of brand affinity, they are likely to come back and purchase again. Of those who have made two purchases from a brand, 45 percent will purchase again, while 66 percent of those who have purchased five times will purchase again. A customer's value to the brand increases more than nine times from their first purchase to the 12th, where they finally demonstrate brand fidelity and evangelism.[7]

What Grow refers to as the Brand Affinity Hierarchy provides the basis for what I call the "New Sales Funnel" of the Elevated Economy. The traditional funnel that you can find in most business school textbooks today has six steps. You start by making your customers aware of your product or service; you then try to take their awareness into interest; from there you do what you can to turn interest into consideration, consideration into intent, intent into evaluation, and evaluation into a purchase. This is the traditional, postwar playbook. As long as the asset leaves your warehouse and makes it into a customer's shopping cart (whether physical or digital), you have done your job. But in the Elevated Economy, a seventh step is added to the funnel, one that goes past the purchase altogether.

This seventh step is obsession. It's dedication. It's loyalty. Or, as Grow puts it, it's evangelism. This is the true end of the sales funnel in the Elevated Economy. You won't be able to win just by selling

---

7 Ibid.

lots of things anymore. Your company is no longer in the selling business. The product you want is the heart of the customer, and the currency you need to acquire it is your brand. Your company must be a brand and not just a product or service in this decade and those to come.

This seventh step is not the end of the old sales funnel; it's the goal of an entirely new model that certain analysts are starting to call the "Hourglass Model" of modern sales. This model adds six new phases that begin as soon as the traditional funnel ends. Purchase in the hourglass model does not end with a purchase. A purchase is merely the halfway point.

In the hourglass model, after a consumer makes a purchase, it becomes time to implement the second set of phases. They are:

1. **Activation:** The moment your customer makes their first purchase is no time to abandon them and start again at the top of the funnel. Doing so leaves huge buying potential on the table. Instead, the moment of purchase should also be the moment of activation. Your firm should have offerings and strategies ready to draw that customer into a much bigger world for your brand. The purchase isn't the end of a customer; it's the beginning of an evangelist.

2. **Repeated Purchase:** In the hourglass model, single purchases are not the goal. Dedicated brand loyalty is. And so, after you begin your activation strategies at the moment of initial purchase, a second purchase is required to determine which customers are proceeding through your second funnel toward advocacy.

3. **Preference:** It is not enough to convince a customer to make one, two, or even many purchases with your firm. In the hourglass

model, the goal is to market, connect, and communicate with your customer to the point that your brand is not just a purchase they make, but a value they hold. They don't just happen to choose your brand; they decide to choose your brand.

4. **Loyalty:** Loyalty is the metric that determines how successful your firm is at creating preferential consumer behavior. Firms that don't already have some type of loyalty metric, and a system to capture it, should strongly consider doing so sooner rather than later.

5. **Referral/Endorsement:** When a customer spreads the word about a product or service, or reviews or endorses that product or service, the firm benefits from word-of-mouth marketing, sometimes referred to as earned media (as opposed to paid media/advertising). This is one of the most valuable customers you can have.

6. **Advocacy:** This is the final step of the hourglass model and the ultimate goal of firms in the Elevated Economy. The winners here will not be the companies with the most customers; they will be those that are able to most consistently turn those customers into committed, consistent purchasers who consider your brand one of many positive expressions of his or her own identity. Reaching this stage takes more time, resources, and intentionality than the pure asset-distribution model of days gone by. But the rewards to both your company's reputation and its bottom line are more than worth the effort when the buyer becomes the seller.

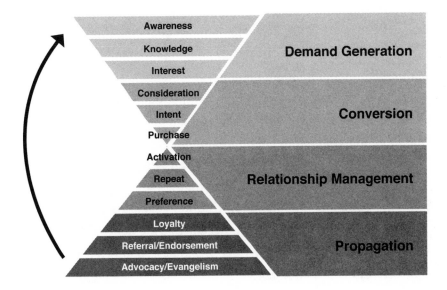

Irma Wallace of SearchRank—a global sales and marketing consultancy—shared her firm's research into the value of an activated advocate. According to their findings:

- 92 percent of customers trust recommendations from people they know.

- Advocates tell twice as many people about their purchases.

- Word-of-mouth recommendations drive 20 to 50 percent of all purchasing decisions.

- Advocates are five times more valuable than average customers because they spend more on products and increase product purchases.

- Customers referred by other customers have a 37 percent higher retention rate.

- Advocates are two to three times more effective than non-advocates when it comes to persuading others to make purchases.
- A 12 percent increase in advocacy generates a 200 percent increase in revenue growth rate.

The path to maximal profitability is changing in the Elevated Economy. Time and resources spent creating customers will not yield stronger results than a focus on activating and cultivating advocates. Firms need to begin considering which strategy they are prioritizing and what pivots they may need to make to place themselves back atop the ever-shifting sands of consumer behavior.

A TRILLION REASONS TO TRY

So which brands do this best today and what can be learned from their examples?

According to the customer research company Brand Keys' annual Customer Loyalty Leaders List for 2019, the top five companies with the most measurable brand loyalty among their customer bases were, from least to most: Netflix, Apple, Samsung, Google, and Amazon. The survey breaks down loyalty based on specific product and service categories. As a result, Amazon notably appears on this ranking twice, once for its tablet sales business and once for its ecommerce service overall. Amazon is, by far, the poster child for customer loyalty, so it's worth taking a moment to examine a few of its key strategies and the results they bring.

 B _k_ R _e_ A _y_ N _s_ D.

Brand Keys Customer Loyalty Leaders List 2019

BRAND	CATEGORY	2019	2018
Amazon	Online Retail	1	1
Google	Search Engines	2	2
Samsung	Smartphones	3	6
Amazon	Tablets	4	9
Apple	Tablets	5	7
Netflix	Video Streaming	6	4
Amazon	Video Streaming	7	5
Apple	Smartphones	8	3
Trader Joe's	Natural Foods	9	10
Hyundai	Automotive	10	14
Twitter	Social Networking	11	23
WhatsApp	Instant Messaging	12	11
Chick-fil-A	Fast Casual Restaurants	13	24
Dunkin' Donuts	Coffee	14	19
Domino's	Pizza	15	12
Ford	Automotive	16	15
Nike	Athletic Footwear	17	18
Discover	Credit Cards	18	26
Avis	Car Rental	19	21
Toyota	Automotive	20	22
PayPal	Online Payments	21	25
Instagram	Social Networking	22	16
iTunes	Video Streaming	23	17
Facebook	Social Networking	24	8
Apple	Computers	25	20

Source: Brand Keys Customer Loyalty Leaders List 2019

The Brand Keys 23rd Annual Loyalty Leaders List of the loyalty rankings for the top 25 brands, out of the 921 brands we assessed in a cross-category analysis of 110 industry categories in the 2019 Brand Keys Customer Loyalty Engagement Index.

Amazon began 2020 with more than 112 million Prime members in the United States.[8] What makes Amazon so much more than a simple online store is Prime and the data it provides. With Prime, Amazon's leadership no longer has to wonder if their customers are advocates; they can figure out exactly how many they have with the push of a button. Amazon asks its more than 112 million US Prime customers to pay an annual fee, usually around $100 or more, to

---

8 https://fortune.com/2020/01/16/amazon-prime-subscriptions/.

take advantage of the features that, for most people, are what make Amazon, Amazon.

Prime members have access to free shipping, special discounts, and exclusive products and services, including music and video. Prime has become the definitive Amazon experience. If you don't have it, you're not really experiencing the key value proposition of the company. Or, to put it another way, unless you are willing to make a monetary statement of brand loyalty, you don't actually get to use the "real" Amazon. Fifteen years ago, this model was something of a novelty, used by the likes of Costco. But today, subscription businesses are booming in the wake of the accelerating value of generating customer loyalty. The strategy is certainly paying off for Amazon, and all that success is a strong indicator of just how much the idea of loyalty is changing in the emerging Elevated Economy.

According to a study from Bain and Company, increasing customer retention by just 5 percent can boost profits anywhere from 25 to 95 percent. That is a powerful multiplier, especially when you consider these facts aggregated from multiple recent articles and studies concerning Amazon's success as a customer loyalty juggernaut:[9]

- 95 percent of Prime members say they would "definitely" or "probably" renew their memberships.

- 85 percent of Prime shoppers visit Amazon at least once a week or more; that number drops to 56 percent for non-Prime members going to Amazon at least once a week.

- 59 percent of shoppers across 27 countries bought items on Amazon.com last year.

---

9   https://hbswk.hbs.edu/archive/the-economics-of-e-loyalty.

- 46 percent of Prime members say they buy on Amazon at least once a week.
- 43 percent of all online sales come from Amazon.
- 31 percent of Prime members go to amazon.com daily.[10]

These facts combined with Bain and Company's multiplier have created unprecedented success for Amazon—enough to help it reach a $1 trillion market capitalization. That's a lot of customer loyalty. That's a lot of votes being cast in Amazon's favor. And that's a lot of proof that businesses in the Elevated Economy should capture the buying behaviors of their customers and transition them into loyal, consistent purchasers and advocates.

The potential for success with this strategy is far too high to ignore.

---

10 https://marketingland.com/85-prime-members-say-visit-amazon-least-week-nearly-13-daily-users-231866.

CHAPTER 9

MORE POWERFUL THAN A LOCOMOTIVE

Seek peace, and pursue it.
—Psalm 34:14

O ne of my favorite traditions with my kids is the "Jar of Questions."

This is exactly what it sounds like. I have dozens of slips of paper in a mason jar in the kitchen. At dinner, I'll open the jar, select a question, and ask them if they have an answer. My kids are young but these are not young questions. We burned through favorite colors and foods years ago. Kids, like consumers, are starting to ask much larger questions than that.

One night with the Question Jar stands out in particular. Written on the slip of paper I pulled out was "What's the biggest problem?"

The question didn't specify if I was asking about problems in our country, in the world, or just in our house. It didn't ask about the biggest problem at their school, or something they personally don't like. I was curious to hear, from the unfiltered minds of my children, what single issue was reigning supreme above all the other problems they'd been made aware of in their very few years on this earth.

To my immense surprise, neither of my children missed a beat. Almost immediately my eldest, born in 2009, explained that to her, the most concerning issue she knew about was climate change. I couldn't remember ever explicitly explaining the consequences of climate change to my daughter in full. And yet, here she was, in a completely ego-less environment, expressing honestly that to her, even as a young child, the future of the planet's ability to sustain her life was her greatest concern.

All children have anxieties, but this is the first generation to have to worry about the future of the environment on such a large scale. The members of my children's generation seem to be more informed, and as a result, more concerned than previous ones.

This change in mindset represents one of the most important economic factors that we can measure today. In just a decade and a half, my children and others like them will be the new economic inheritors. Millennials and Gen Z are already moving progressively in this direction, but my daughter's generation is the first to be born into it naturally. The economic ramifications of a change in mindset this extreme are highly significant and worth the attention of any professional who wants to have a hand in guiding the organizations of today into tomorrow.

Consumers have their own jar of questions. In the past, the majority of those questions were connected primarily to basic buying power. How much is it? Where can I get one? Is it a quality product or service?

But in the Elevated Economy, the questions in the jars of new consumers are going to be quite different. They will no longer ask: What does this product cost to buy? They will instead ask: What was the cost of creating it in the first place? Instead of: How do I get it? It will be: Is this being delivered to me in an environmentally conscious way? And instead of: Is this a quality product or service? It will be: Does this product or service allow for the highest quality of life—both for myself as a consumer, and for all the stakeholders involved?

A massive migration is happening. Historically marginalized groups are becoming cornerstones—customer bases for new and emerging businesses. Cornerstones that aren't built on geographical or socioeconomic bullet points, but are built on the foundational identity of each consumer. A recent article in *The Economist* puts it like this:

> On reflection, it seems obvious that cultural change can unlock the economic potential of people and ideas, with history-altering results. Such shifts matter for reasons other than their effect on GDP. Evolving norms that allow women, ethnic minorities, immigrants, and gay and transgender people to play full roles in society not only boost growth but reduce human suffering. But because these shifts matter economically, the dismal science needs a better understanding of when and how cultures change—especially now.[1]

It is not a coincidence that Bezos and his contemporaries in the Business Council are already signaling their willingness to comply with this new mindset. These leaders pay too many experts too much money to be caught unaware when the tide begins to recede. They know this wave is coming. And they're preparing for it.

Are you? What changes have you made to be more inclusive,

---

1   https://www.economist.com/finance-and-economics/2019/07/25/a-societys-values-and-beliefs-matter-for-its-economy.

combat racism, address climate change, fix pay inequality, and ensure your vendors and suppliers are being treated fairly?

A recent paper titled "Paradigm Shifts in Economic Theory and Policy" by Laurie Laybourn-Langton and Michael Jacobs from London's Institute for Public Policy Research delves deeply into the connections between people's buying identities and their everyday identities. According to the paper:

> Politico-economic paradigms can exert a powerful influence over academic and media debates, as well as on policymaking institutions, both national and international. Over the last hundred years, Western political economy has broadly experienced two major periods of breakdown and transition from one politico-economic paradigm to another.
>
> The first was from the laissez-faire paradigm to the post-war consensus, covering the period from the Wall Street Crash of 1929 to the implementation of mainly Keynesian economic orthodoxy and policy approaches in the post-war period. The second was from the post-war consensus to neoliberalism, starting with the currency and oil shocks of the early 1970s and the adoption of free market economic policies in the 1980s, ushering in the current period of neoliberalism.[2]

As each of these shifts came to pass, the line between what we buy and who we are becomes more blurred. What I call the Elevated Economy is the third of these transitions. Triggered by an explosion of connectivity, convenience, and awareness powered by the Internet,

---

2 "Paradigm Shifts in Economic Theory and Policy," *Intereconomics* (Hamburg), vol. 53, no. 3 (May 2018): 113–118, https://search.proquest.com/openview/8d548e3c67b3465 c8d4e9f125057e51e.

this third shift has blurred that line nearly beyond recognition. In the Elevated Economy, who you are and what you buy are virtually one and the same.

The best way you as a business leader can avoid being similarly obscured by this worldwide paradigm shift is to get up, quickly, and move. The P of place used to deal mostly with the physical (and then digital) location of your business. But the most relevant land grab happening now in the modern economy is happening within the minds and identities of the new consumers. With the Internet, you can sell anything to anyone anywhere. And so, what matters most now is not how close your business's store is to my house, it's how close your business's identity is to either my own or the one I aspire to.

Placing your business in this sort of context is challenging, but it becomes infinitely easier the faster you act. In the Elevated Economy—an age of commerce defined by technology and all of the convenience and potential for self-expression that comes along with it—customers won't connect with you because they walked by your signs. They will connect with you because you walk side by side with them, helping them express their identity. That journey, like any other, begins with a single step.

PLACE AUDIT: BLOCKBUSTED

Outside of our friends at the IRS, the word *audit* doesn't need to be an instrument of fear. Business leaders love a good audit. You can only influence or improve your business if you know where it stands. You have to know where to begin before you can determine where to go.

Positioning a business to ensure positive performance within the Elevated Economy is no different. But before beginning the audit and making your plan, it's important to understand the consequences that could happen if you don't. The Elevated Economy is like a freight train. Right now, we can only hear the whistle blaring in the distance. But it's getting louder. It's getting closer. But some of us have not heard it, or have chosen to ignore what is happening altogether.

If we zoom out on the metaphorical track just a bit, we can see the train itself as well as all the bodies littered behind it. One of the most famous is Blockbuster. The once-undisputed champion of at-home entertainment was infamously usurped to the point of bankruptcy by Netflix and online video streaming. The story has become one of business history's most famous punch lines, but one key detail is often missed among all the others.

Unlike other category-defining companies that fell into failure like Enron in the 1990s, Blockbuster's implosion was not a result of borderline unethical cost-cutting, dishonest business practices, or outright criminality. Blockbuster failed not by its actions, but by its inaction. The whistle of rapidly changing consumer behavior was blaring, but the company refused to react. This is the sort of corporate apathy that can reduce a seemingly unstoppable juggernaut to a blue-and-yellow smudge on the tracks.

Blockbuster's leadership team were not fools, however. They simply chose to bet on the wrong horse. They were faced with the same choice all business leaders have to make as the Elevated Economy speeds toward them: Do we move quickly to evolve our organization into one that will thrive with the consumers of tomorrow—even if it costs time and resources today? Or, do we double down on the business we already have—which may be very sound—and trust that it will sustain us through the change?

The choice is not as simple as hindsight typically makes us believe. Trying to anticipate consumer behavior is like trying to shoot a bullet with another bullet. For some, the risk isn't worth the reward. According to a case study about Blockbuster's collapse in *Drift*:

When you dig into the Netflix vs. Blockbuster story, it becomes clear that Blockbuster did (eventually) realize that the Netflix model was the future. And they did make changes to address it.

But in the end, it was too little, too late.

Blockbuster could never fully evolve into the modern business it needed to be in order to compete with Netflix.

. . . Technologies improve. Industries change. In order to grow, you need to keep a pulse on the ever-evolving needs and preferences of your customers so you can make changes to your model accordingly.

This applies to products and services as well as to marketing strategies.[3]

Or, as *Forbes* put it, "The irony is that Blockbuster failed because its leadership had built a well-oiled operational machine. It was a very tight network that could execute with extreme efficiency, but poorly suited to let in new information." This allergy to new information is what ultimately sank Blockbuster. By the time the company allowed reality to sink in, it was already sunk.

The audit process is meant to help leaders make an honest assessment of their companies' current relationship to the immense shift in buying habits that has already begun and will become immutable as the Elevated Economy continues to take greater and greater hold. The questions and steps are meant to help leaders understand if—like Blockbuster—they may be at risk as a result of their own success and previous ingenuity.

Inaction is not an option and speed is of the essence. It may be difficult to remake what you've already built, but doing so should be far more palatable than scrubbing its remains off the grill of a runaway locomotive.

---

3 https://www.drift.com/blog/netflix-vs-blockbuster/.

PLACE AUDIT: ENVIRONMENTAL IMPACT

The Elevated Economy is unique because it represents a moment where, for the first time in human history, a statistically significant number of people are willing to actively shift their buying decisions away from products they believe are good, to corporations they believe DO good. Never before has the moral standing of a firm been more important or relevant to its own success. The primary barometer these new consumers use to judge whether a company fits into their identity-driven economic determinations is built on three major pillars: environmental effort, logistical virtue, and sociological footprint.

Environmental effort is a carefully chosen phrase. It's important to note that consumers in the Elevated Economy do not only support companies that are actively planting trees in the rain forest or stripping carbon from the atmosphere. Instead, what they are looking for is effort. They are asking, "Is this company taking *any* efforts to secure the future of my planet?"

If the answer is no, that's a major problem.

Drew Fraser, CEO of Method Products, says his company takes this seriously—to the point where they have dedicated staff positions known as "greenskeepers." According to Fraser:

> We have a set of rules that are not only about the ingredients but the practices that we expect our suppliers to adhere to. And we have folks in our organization and we call them greenskeepers, and that's their life, and they wake up every day with a deep, scientific, and strategic knowledge of what we're trying to accomplish from a sustainability standpoint. And they bring that to life. They work closely with our product engineers, our manufacturing and our project managers, and our formulators

and our fragrance people, and work together to make sure the products that we're building are as green as they can be.[4]

It is rapidly becoming a legitimate competitive advantage to be seen as an ecologically friendly corporation. A recent Nielsen study titled "How and Why Sustainability Is Gaining Momentum with Consumers" contains some highly compelling evidence to the increasingly fundamental intersection between capitalism and conservatism. The study took a look at three standard consumer goods: chocolate, coffee, and bath products. Its goal was to determine whether brands within these categories with active and noticeable efforts to communicate environmental effort to their consumers performed more favorably than their seemingly non-sustainable counterparts. The results are fairly striking.

According to the report:

> For all three categories, dollar sales of items with the specific claims studied grew twice as fast as the weighted average dollar growth of the three categories combined. In other words, products with certain sustainability attributes outperformed the growth rate of total products in their respective categories despite challenges that might have predicted otherwise, like a relatively smaller market share.[5]

Chocolate sales, specifically, produced significant spikes in performance when coupled with pro-environmental claims. As stated in the study:

---

4   Fraser, discussion with author.

5   https://www.nielsen.com/us/en/insights/article/2018/sustainability-sells-linking-sustainability-claims-to-sales/.

While chocolate with environmental claims makes up only 0.2% of the total category share, it grew by 22% from March 2017 to March 2018. This is more than 4x the rate of total category dollar growth when it comes to sales. Looking at units, it's a similar story: We see chocolate with environmental claims flying off the shelves at a rate 5x faster than the overall market—15% unit sales growth compared with 3%.

Sales of products with fair trade claims (which make up only 0.1% of total chocolate share) are growing faster than the overall category as well, with dollar sales growth outpacing category growth by 2x (10% vs. 5%) and unit sales growth by 5x (15% vs. 3%).[6]

To conclude, the study drew a strong correlation between the presence of pro-sustainability messaging and growth for each of the three product areas. It also points out the newness of this sort of analysis while calling for more robust measurement practices with which to further channel its potential impact:

> In many ways this space is evolving; however, what we do know is that sustainability presents an opportunity to be creative about innovative growth. Embedding consumer demand for sustainability into your company strategy and product pipeline requires data specific to your brand footprint and consumer profile.[7]

Measurement is the key missing piece here for most of the attributes that make up the Elevated Economy, and this has been true for

---

6   Ibid.

7   Ibid.

each of the other major transitions in consumer behavior as well. The ESG measurement firm MSCI notes:

> From natural resource scarcity to changing governance standards, from global workforce management to the evolving regulatory landscape, ESG factors can impact the long-term risk and return profile of institutional portfolios. MSCI ESG Ratings are designed to help investors to understand ESG risks and opportunities and integrate these factors into their portfolio construction and management process.
>
> Our global team of experienced research analysts assesses thousands of data points across 37 ESG Key Issues, focusing on the intersection between a company's core business and the industry issues that can create significant risks and opportunities for the company. Companies are rated on a AAA-CCC scale relative to the standards and performance of their industry peers.[8]

MSCI attempts to quantify ESG by aiming to answer the following questions:

> Of the negative externalities that companies in an industry generate, which issues may turn into unanticipated costs for companies in the medium to long term? Conversely, which ESG issues affecting an industry may turn into opportunities for companies in the medium to long term? More specifically, the MSCI ESG Ratings model seeks to answer four key questions about companies:

---

8   All quotes from MSCI come from this source: https://www.msci.com/
documents/1296102/14524248/MSCI+ESG+Ratings+Methodology+-
+Exec+Summary+2019.pdf/2dfcaeee-2c70-d10b-69c8-
3058b14109e3?t=1571404887226.

- What are the most significant ESG risks and opportunities facing a company and its industry?

- How exposed is the company to those key risks and/or opportunities?

- How well is the company managing key risks and opportunities?

- What is the overall picture for the company and how does it compare to its global industry peers?[9]

Measurement is difficult, but some standardization currently exists—courtesy of none other than the United Nations and Ben & Jerry's.

PLACE AUDIT: MULTI-CAPITALISM AS THE NEW GOLDEN METRIC

The legendary ice cream duo may seem like a strange choice to lead any sort of corporate revolution, but Ben & Jerry's has recently become the sharp end of the spear for a new form of business measurement called "multi-capitalism."

Measuring ESG success is one of the biggest challenges companies may face when attempting to join the Elevated Economy. How can you possibly measure the impact of more recycling bins or increased time off against all the many other outstanding concerns relevant to a healthy business?

Multi-capitalism is, as the name suggests, an attempt to get corporations to care about and begin to measure the success of their organizations on many forms of capital, not just monetary. This can

---

9 Ibid.

include social, environmental, or societal capital. These new factors all add up to three new bottom lines for your company.

In addition to an economic or financial bottom line, multi-capitalism adds social and environmental bottom lines to your basic reporting structure as well. Determining holistic success, therefore, becomes dependent on the success of all three bottom lines rather than the single success metric most business leaders have spent their careers chasing. This is a radical departure, but a necessary one if corporations want to accurately understand their alignment with the demands of the Elevated Economy. Without these insights, your organization will be as susceptible to the whims of economic evolution as a sailboat without an anchor is to those of the wind.

The official one-pager on multi-capitalism from Thomas & McElroy LLC puts things in greater context. It states that:

> Capital theory in the sustainability and economics literature expresses the view that there are five broad categories of capital: natural, human, social & relationship, constructed and economic. Included in economic capital is financial or monetary capital; and included in human, social and relationship, constructed and economic capitals is intellectual capital. Organizational performance, then, can and should be thought of in terms of impacts on all vital capital relative to norms, standards or thresholds for what they would have to be in order to be sustainable. Value, it turns out, is by no means restricted to economic assets.
>
> ... As a doctrine, Multi-Capitalism is the evolutionary result of Context-Based Sustainability (CBS), a methodology initially devised for non-financial management only. What's new and exciting about Multi-Capitalism, therefore, is its extension of CBS into the financial domain and to organizational

performance more broadly construed. Multi-Capitalism, that is, finally makes integrated Triple Bottom Line management possible. This changes everything.[10]

Triple Bottom Line Management is a crucial component for success in the Elevated Economy, and complying with its precepts means embracing a new sort of scorecard for your business. As published in the *Harvard Business Review*, the multi-capitalist scorecard is perhaps the most powerful and effective reporting structure for companies looking to thrive in the Elevated Economy.

According to Kris Miller, eBay has adopted programs that reflect these three bottom lines, even if they weren't created with them specifically in mind. She told me in a recent interview that:

We have a really great program called Retail Revival, where we actually go into smaller cities, in the US but also in other countries. We adopt brick-and-mortar stores within those cities and towns for a full year. We dedicate a ton of resources to helping the brick-and-mortar stores within those communities learn how to become an online seller. It's amazing, the number of brick-and-mortar small businesses that are not online. We dedicate tons of people-hours to teach them how to have a thriving online business. It's been very successful.

One of my favorite stories is from a gentleman from Akron, Ohio. He made enough money once he came through the eBay program to actually start a whole second business, which I think is

---

10   Martin P. Thomas and Mark W. McElroy, *The MultiCapital Scorecard: Rethinking Organizational Performance* (White River Junction, VT: Chelsea Green Publishing, 2016).

amazing. So, it's helping people thrive. It's also creating communities within those communities of eBay buyers and sellers where they may have not met each other before or worked together. And then the other part of it is that the local government is very much involved. So, the city council and the mayor, and those small businesses, now have relationships with their local government, which also helps the community thrive. So, it's been a nice win-win-win across the board. It's a microcosm of what the eBay platform does in a much broader sense around the world.[11]

Strategies like this demonstrate just how dynamic multi-capitalist thinking can be in practice.

PLACE AUDIT: SCORING YOUR MULTI-CAPITAL

The multi-capitalism scorecard breaks each of the three bottom lines into subcategories. These subcategories make understanding your company's relationship to multi-capitalism—and, by extension, its predicted strength within the new consumer context of the Elevated Economy—much simpler. Measuring your performance in each of these categories is the key to understanding how much further you may or may not need to bring your firm to truly thrive in the coming decades.

Social Category 1—Living Wage: Does your company offer wages to its lowest-paid employees capable of paying for basic expenses and/or the basic expenses of an entire family?

---

11 Miller, discussion with author.

Social Category 2—Workplace Safety: Does your company provide a place where employees are protected physically, emotionally, and economically?

Social Category 3—Innovative Capacity: Is your company actively inspiring its employees and providing pathways to production for new ideas and strategies?

Economic Category 1—Equity: What is your company's income?

Economic Category 2—Borrowing: What are your company's debts?

Economic Category 3—Competitive Practices: How well does your company perform against its competitors?

Environmental Category 1—Water Supplies: How does your company impact the watersheds of its physical environment and of the physical environments it practically impacts?

Environmental Category 2—Solid Wastes: What does your company do with the waste it creates?

Environmental Category 3—The Climate System: What impact does your company have on the climate or other macro-environmental factors?

Performance in each of these categories is aggregated into a single performance indicator—one that is invaluable to success in the Elevated Economy. Measuring your success in each can be varied and subjective, but the result cannot. Whether your firm embraces this particular scoring system or another, the writing on the wall remains clear. The days of a single bottom line are numbered. If you want to appropriately position your company in the Elevated Economy and become the sort of firm that consumers, investors, and employees will connect with, then you must embrace some form of multi-capitalism and set up a reporting system to track your success and advocate for improvements.

Doing so is the only way to know for certain if you are going to be stuck on the tracks or riding in the slipstream by the time the train arrives.

CHAPTER 10

THE HOLE IN THE UNIVERSE

"Life is very simple, but we insist on making it complicated."
—Confucius

One of my professors in business school had a knack for rapid prioritization. In just a sentence or two, he could get a class full of naive students with visions of sprawling empires and scrappy upstarts running through their heads to snap their idealism into reality. One of his questions has stuck with me: "If your business disappeared in an instant, who would miss it?"

I thought the professor was encouraging us to build companies and leave behind a legacy of business success, regardless of how we achieved that success. But now, with the benefit of hindsight, I realize how wrong I was.

Take someone like Mark Zuckerberg, for example. Like Bill Gates and Microsoft before him, initially Zuckerberg's robotic demeanor created a smokescreen of nerdy charm that blocked the world from seeing the ambition lurking behind his unblinking eyes. Look at any interview or publicly available depositions that the young CEO gave during Facebook's initial ascendance and you'll see just how ruthless he was. Young founders like Gates and Zuckerberg began their empires by chasing success, power, and total dominance.

Today, Bill Gates and Mark Zuckerberg, in addition to their massive business successes, are the heads of two of the largest charities in the world. The headlines they create have transitioned from sly winks at their own success, to earnest pleas for better environmental practices and easier access to clean drinking water in the developing world.

Perhaps this is best exemplified by a 2013 article in *Forbes* in which Warren Buffett, a lion in the world of finance, accepting a philanthropic award, said:

> The truth is I have never given a penny away that had any utility to me. . . . I am very grateful for this award; I accept this award. But I'd like to accept it not only for myself but for those millions of people who really give away money that's important to them because they see somebody else where they think they can do more good.[1]

Buffett concluded with a message for those who haven't yet taken his Giving Pledge, a commitment by billionaires to give away at least half of their fortune during their lives or when they pass: "If you have trouble living on $500 million, I'm gonna put out a book, *How to Live on $500 Million*. Think about whether the other $500 million might do more for humanity than it will for you and your family."[2]

---

1   https://www.forbes.com/sites/randalllane/2013/06/06/bonos-moving-serenade-of-warren-buffett-video/#5b17d4637732.

2   https://www.forbes.com/sites/randalllane/2013/11/18/the-50-philanthropists-who-have-given-away-the-most-money/#20efa23d1f5a.

If you look, you'll see this arc playing out over and over again as more and more of the "Tech 2.0" CEOs who fought their way out of the dot-com crash and became business legends, have turned their thoughts from securing market dominance to securing a legacy. However, even these bright young men and women—the champions of a brilliant age of online innovation—are being outpaced by an ever newer and younger group of business leaders who are building very powerful businesses for an entirely new generation of consumers. And they are doing so by following the good practices of the financial lions before them.

Companies that are beginning to win and will continue to win in the burgeoning Elevated Economy are going about their business very differently than the Gateses or Zuckerbergs of days past. Rather than starting out by being ruthless, cold, and calculating and then transitioning into becoming compassionate and altruistic, the new class of leadership is leading with compassion, purpose, and some degree of altruism. Companies—big companies, world-changing companies—are incorporating the good of the planet, humanity, and posterity into their businesses from the very beginning.

This is the essence of marketing and advertising in the Elevated Economy. In the past, telling the story of your business meant doing a ton of research to try and figure out what customers want and then telling them all the ways your product or service will solve that problem. But in the Elevated Economy, things have changed. Now the attention has shifted from the product or service and onto the corporation itself.

If you found yourself back in 2002 and asked a group of 10 strangers what they thought of Google, you would get answers ranging from "I love how simple it is" to "I love how colorful and fun their logo is." But bring Google up today, especially in certain circles, and you're much more likely to hear responses along the lines of "I hear they treat their employees pretty rough," or "I don't like that they are willing to censor their services if it lets them enter the Chinese market."

You would still hear plenty about the great services and clever branding that Google creates and employs, but the conversation has changed enough to demand our attention. One article from *Wired* titled "What Backlash?" explains that the favorability index for all the major FAANG players is still shockingly high. The article explains that:

> Amazon, Facebook, and Google have all held steady in daily favorability polls conducted by research firm Morning Consult over the past year. The ratings wiggle a bit from week to week, but the companies haven't seen any decline. 88 percent of respondents view Google favorably, compared with only 6 percent who hold a negative view. Morning Consult calls this a "net favorability" of 82 percent. By the same measure, Amazon is at 77 percent, and Facebook sits at 60 percent.[3]

These numbers are interesting, but what's truly remarkable is that articles like this, and the research that powers them, even exist at all. Nobody in the 1950s had an opinion about Maytag outside of the convenience of a cold fridge, where they could buy one, and how much it would cost. But today, the Maytag Man, once called "the loneliest man in the world" (because the machines never needed repairing or replacing), would face greater scrutiny as a representative of a brand. These days, statistics would have to prove his worth, instead of the pleasant, folksy images presented by advertisers and trusted by consumers without investigation and research. Today, companies have to prove themselves.

My professor had it right all those years back. You can't just think

---

3 https://www.wired.com/story/what-tech-backlash-google-facebook-still-rank-high-in-polls/.

about how the world will be with your business in it anymore. You have to think instead of how the world will be without you in it at all. He called this concept "the hole in the universe," and back then, I would have sided with Zuckerberg and Gates. I would have thought that the hole in the universe is something that businesses fill with their big ideas and successful product lines. But it isn't.

Elevated business leaders are not attempting to build monuments to their own success, they are trying to provide value to the human race long after they are gone.

In the Elevated Economy, consumers don't just want to know what you sell, they want to know who you are. This is a massive shift in the core philosophies that have governed the creation and distribution of assets for generations. The goal of marketing for businesses is no longer to answer what you sell, how much it costs, or where to find it. In fact, the primary concern of every marketing department in the Elevated Economy should be just a single question.

Why?

WHY-POWERED MARKETING IN THE ELEVATED ECONOMY

Joe Biden noticed and drew attention to the rapidly evolving business landscape via an op-ed. Liberal politicians are more likely to chide than champion the "big business" community, but Biden was nearly gushing when he wrote about its changing culture:

> We see Larry Fink, who oversees trillions in wealth at BlackRock, call on companies to act in the best interests of their communities, not just shareholders.
>
> We've seen CEOs acting once again as part of communities,

not apart from communities. Taking stands on guns and on LGBTQ rights. There is a whole movement of the leading CEOs to begin to change the corporate culture and acknowledge they have responsibilities in the communities in which they live. There is a new movement to begin to change the corporate culture, which in my view, and theirs, has gotten out of whack in the past 25 years.

We've seen business leaders stand up for sound immigration policies, and stand up for human rights in the process. Business is leading again. And I applaud CEOs around the country for pushing change forward.

I have never been more optimistic in my entire career than I am today. I have never been more optimistic about America's ability to lead the world—politically, economically, militarily—than I am today.[4]

The transition he is explaining here, minus the folksy political parlance, is the Elevated Economy in brief. It is a migration of the governing business principles from the original four P's to include the new P of purpose. The way a business conducts itself is now more important than it has ever been in the entire history of capitalism. Things like price and place are still vitally important elements, but for the next generation of consumers, the new fifth P edges them out just slightly in terms of overall importance.

Marketing, at its best, was always designed to answer questions for customers by connecting them to one of the original four P's. Are you creating a line of budget-conscious fishing gear to help hobbyists

---

4   https://bidenforum.org/geography-can-shape-opportunity-joe-biden-wants-to-change-that-1617d07f02c6.

get out on the water easier? Your marketing should probably focus on how much money the consumer will save if they choose you over a competitor. Are you launching a new art gallery downtown? Your marketing should probably be focusing on finding and educating local customers about your location, events, and so on.

In the late 1990s and early 2000s, marketing evolved by demanding that just about every business on the planet focus on the P of place. "Are you online?" was a question that store owners and salespeople began to hear over and over and over again. It didn't matter if you were an art gallery or a fishing gear distributor anymore. Just about every piece of marketing material going anywhere at that time featured a big fat dot-com somewhere on the page.

The Elevated Economy is creating a similar groundswell for today's marketing efforts that the Internet did in years past. This is why you see car companies today advertising their environmental conservationism. It's why your cloud service provider is telling you about their commitment to climate action. It's why you see commercials from companies willing to shell out multiple millions per minute just for the chance to say "we value the things that you value, we are taking a stand too."

The Internet got customers to start asking one question above all else: Can I use the web to interact with your business? If the answer was no, you were out of luck. In the Elevated Economy, consumers are once again bubbling a single question up to the top. They want to know "why."

Business analyst Daniel Yankelovich theorizes that this is the product of the era in which we live. Yankelovich's research has led him to identify what he calls the three waves of consumer mistrust. The first was triggered by the Great Depression in the '30s, the second began as economic malaise and political upheaval gripped the United

States during the Vietnam War in the '60s and didn't end until Ronald Reagan tempted Americans back to their shopping carts with visions of two-car garages and aboveground pools. Finally, the third was triggered by the dot-com bust in the very early 2000s and is still very much a part of our current economic culture.

Yankelovich summarized his findings in a plea for updated success metrics for businesses titled "Making Trust a Competitive Asset: Breaking Out of Narrow Frameworks." According to an article about the report in *Strategy+Business* magazine:

> Reversing the current wave of mistrust, the authors argue, requires profound changes in both corporate and management attitudes and behavior. Companies must move away from jealously managing corporate image or spinning the truth to influence public opinion and, instead, practice open and honest dialogue to build "trust equity" with the public.[5]

This is perhaps the most fundamental truth of marketing in the Elevated Economy: it is no longer enough to try and figure out what consumers want and try to sell it; now it is your job to figure out what consumers want and try to become it. You can't cheat an Elevated consumer. The lock has fallen off the closet door, and the skeletons that used to live happily within are now just waiting to become company-killing scandals. In order to avoid this, Yankelovich recommends three practical changes:

- Working with Wall Street analysts to develop new performance metrics that quantify a company's trust equity.

---

5   https://www.strategy-business.com/article/04218?gko=80a32.

- Overhauling leadership development programs to reflect the new skills needed by top executives, including the ability to quickly understand the interests of diverse stakeholders—among them, employees, investors, the media, suppliers, communities, non-governmental organizations, and regulators.

- Systematically engaging key employees and stakeholders in strategic dialogues that push people outside their "comfort zones" and encourage them to challenge standard ways of operating.

The ultimate goal of these efforts, according to the report, is for companies to start building a new kind of value, called "trust equity," with their markets. In order to do this, he says:

> They must get beyond a singular focus on maximizing near-term shareholder value no matter the cost to society. Companies need to accept the idea that creating social capital boosts shareholder value in the long run.[6]

Companies in the Elevated Economy are powered by people buying in to their whys, not just buying their wares. There will always be a segment of the population that purchases primarily based on price and convenience, but the big change being made today is that it is no longer feasible to build an empire on the strength of that particular segment alone. You can build a business that strip mines for cheap diamonds, but you will have a hard time building a scaled chain of jewelry stores without having a better answer to your customers' "why."

In particular, there are three "Why questions" that businesses can

---

6 Ibid.

and should be devoting their marketing resources to answer if they want to connect to consumers in the Elevated Economy.

1. WHY ARE YOU IN BUSINESS?

"Create an everything store," "Connect the world," "Organize the earth's information"—these are the one-line corporate credos of Amazon, Facebook, and Google, respectively. If these corporations were represented solely by a flag, these phrases would be translated into Latin and emblazoned across them. If a reporter asks their CEOs, their answers will be along these lines. But if a board member asks, the line may be quite different. We have no way of knowing for sure, but even if their commitment to such lofty ideas is just a front, that commitment still represents a level of interest in and commitment to issues beyond the bottom line. One of the reasons these companies became and remain so popular through scandals, adversity, and competition is because on some subconscious, psychologically foundational level, people may believe that these companies are interested in the interests of others.

Compare that to a company like General Motors. One of the reasons Elon Musk was able to take Tesla from a ridiculous pipe dream to one of the most in-demand automotive brands on earth was because he elevated a commodity market by using altruistic intention. He wasn't just going to give consumers the chance to buy a new car. He was going to give them a chance to buy a new car that could save the world. Tesla has had its fair share of swerves and skids, but it's still in the race. And both Wall Street and Main Street are paying attention.

More and more corporate leaders are amending their corporate bylaws and mission statements to include elevated ideas like fair trade, decent employment, and environmental protection. A study of such leaders produced by Booz Allen Hamilton surveyed hundreds of executives to find out how they viewed the growing value of values. One of the key findings of this study was that:

> Top performers consciously connect values and operations. Companies that report superior financial results emphasize such values as commitment to employees, drive to succeed, and adaptability far more than their peers. They are also more successful in linking values to the way they run their companies: A significantly greater number report that their management practices are effective in fostering values that influence growth, and executives at these companies are more likely to believe that social and environmental responsibility have a positive effect on financial performance.[7]

Wanting to be a profitable company and wanting to be a company with consciousness are no longer separated by a fork in the road. In fact, the two paths have now merged into one. Succeeding from this point forward will require corporate leaders to define and educate their employees and customers as to how that hole in the universe is made a little smaller by their presence.

2. WHY ARE YOU DOING THAT?

Every action is public now. There is virtually nowhere for companies to hide their sins anymore.

Former Boeing CEO Harry Stonecipher was fired over an affair with an employee; he'd been hired just 15 months earlier to help

---

7 Ibid.

improve Boeing's standing with its largest customer, the Pentagon. A half century earlier, a boardroom discussion about sexual fraternization might have been met with willful ignorance. But in the wake of the Elevated Economy, even our oldest habits are dying hard.

A CEO's sex life has very little to do with the air speed of a 747. But Boeing's board realized that, in the current climate, every decision makes a difference. Consumers are simply too aware and too interested now to risk a cover-up. In the past, such things were "nobody's business." Today, businesses are admitting their mistakes publicly and firing CEOs left, right, and center.

In a study conducted by the global PR firm Cohn and Wolfe, respondents were asked to rank qualities or behaviors that they value most in corporations. Numbers two and three were "not letting customers down" and "acting with integrity at all times." Those two alone are strong indicators that the Elevated Economy already had deep roots within the buying impulses of consumers; but the top spot is even more dramatic. The number one quality or behavior that the respondents wanted to see was: "communicating honestly about products and services."

Above integrity, ethics, and even the environment is honesty. Consumers are ready to pounce on lies but, more importantly, they are ready to reward honesty. Marketing can be a powerful force for honest communication in the Elevated Economy. There's no magic trick or formula for this one. You are either being honest or you're not. But what is guaranteed is that honesty has suddenly shifted from a corporate liability to a competitive advantage. We now live in an age where being more honest than the shop across the street could lead to gains on your balance sheet. If your company is in any position to communicate an honest success or correct a past or current impropriety, it must. And if nobody is saying so around your conference tables, you need to raise your hand.

3. WHY SHOULD I CARE?

This is the final *why* that elevated corporations need to answer for their consumers. It is also arguably the most difficult to quantify and put into practice. Getting consumers to care about and buy what you sell is the goal of marketing. It's challenging to strike the perfect chord with consumers, but the Elevated Economy is a useful tool in finding that chord because it gives leaders a predictable path to generating engagement.

In the past, marketers would ask questions like "How can I get the customer to care about this product?" And the answer to that could be one of a million things. Maybe they like the color red, or the cheap price, or the modern design. That's why ads from the Golden Age of marketing in the 1960s often included three or more paragraphs of text; they had a lot of ground to cover.

In the Elevated Economy, because consumers are now more fully combining their real-world identities with their buying identities, you can build marketing strategies around much larger, but simpler, ideas. A great example of this in action is Impossible Foods.

Impossible Foods uses bleeding-edge technology to create plant-based meat that does the same. They might not contain an ounce of real beef, but Impossible Burgers grill, smell, cook, and bleed just like the real thing. The taste isn't quite the same, but the effort has gone a long way with consumers. The company has raised over $680 million since its founding as it expands its product lines to more restaurants and grocery stores around the world.

I recently had the chance to tour the Impossible Foods headquarters just north of Silicon Valley in Redwood City. I strolled through the fascinating wing of laboratories the company has set up to build and refine its products. I heard from many of the company's leaders, and what struck me most was how little any of them talked about eating.

The marketing is created, the money is raised, and—in many cases—the products are purchased on the strength of what is driving Impossible Foods to do what it does. Impossible's leadership has made it clear that they aren't a burger company. They are an environmental science company.

Impossible Foods CEO Pat Brown's favorite talking points have nothing to do with what makes his burgers "delicious" or "cravable" the way you might expect from hawkers like McDonald's. Instead, Brown is best known for saying things like:

> Today's Impossible Burger requires approximately 75% less water and 95% less land, and generates about 87% lower greenhouse gas emissions than a conventional burger from cows. And while it has the iron and protein, the Impossible Burger is produced without using hormones or antibiotics and contains no cholesterol.[8]

That doesn't exactly sound delicious, but it does sound immensely positive for the environment, and consumers are interested in supporting the company's efforts to turn back the clock on climate change and other environmental crises. In his blog post for the company, Brown writes:

> We're not going to solve this problem by pleading with consumers to eat beans and tofu instead of meat and fish. Even many of

---

8   https://impossiblefoods.com/company/overview/.

the world's most ardent environmentalists, acutely aware of the destructive impact of their diet, continue to eat animals every day.

. . . Over the next few years, the best pork, the best chicken, the best fish, cheese, eggs the world has ever seen will be made directly from plants, using the knowhow and tools Impossible Foods is developing today.[9]

That is how you get people to care about your company in the Elevated Economy—by building a bridge between them, your company, and the things they care about *most*. Most people want clean air and stable weather. Most people want good jobs for themselves and their kids. Most people want the human race to become smarter, safer, and healthier over time. Does your business offer solutions to one or more of *those* problems?

If it does, marketing becomes as simple as spreading the word.

RETURN ON VALUES—ROV

Yankelovich proposed a new metric to measure how well customers are rewarding businesses for being good stewards of these issues. He called it ROV or Return on Values, his thinking being that companies can expect to reap real monetary rewards by fostering values as a way of investment. In his study, he cites Kevin Murray's book *People with Purpose: How Great Leaders Use Purpose to Build Thriving Organizations*:

In a business environment increasingly dominated by attention to definable returns on specific investments, most senior

---

9 https://medium.com/impossible-foods/the-mission-that-motivates-us-d4d7de61665.

executives are surprisingly lax in attempting to quantify a return on values (ROV). Fewer than half say they have the ability to measure a direct link to revenue and earnings growth.[10]

Marketing is just one piece of the puzzle. Telling the story is just the last step. True elevated businesses care about creating real ROV; and they invest in their own ability to measure that success.

"If your business disappeared tomorrow, who would miss it?"

Those words have never been more relevant than they are now.

METHOD PRODUCTS: ELEVATION IN THE WINDY CITY

During my interview with Drew Fraser, he shared a story that aligns perfectly with what it means to "fill the hole in the universe" within the Elevated Economy. In his own words:

There's one example that is as clear as day and it's something that still gives me goosebumps when I think about it. We built our factory on the South Side of Chicago. Previously, we had co-packed our products, but we made a decision that we were going to own the full supply chain—from soil to shelf—and we made a choice to build a factory. Supply chain consultants will tell you that, in the business that we're in, you should build a factory somewhere within around a 50- to 75-mile radius of Chicago; that's where the rails come through. It optimizes the transportation, and for liquid in a bottle, that's very important.

---

10   *People with Purpose: How Great Leaders Use Purpose to Build Thriving Organizations* (London: Kogan Page, 2017), 82.

And what most companies would do is go find a cornfield, cut it down, and build a factory. And what we decided to do was go into the South Side of Chicago, into an area that had exceptionally high unemployment and crime rates, and take on the opportunity to build a factory in the middle of the South Side, bring jobs having an impact on the neighborhood. We hired folks who didn't have bank accounts because they had never been paid before. On their first day of work, we were helping them set up bank accounts so we could pay them and send them their checks. We had rules about no previous training being required and we'd teach you everything you needed to know.

We expanded that model [into] a very violent part of the neighborhood and started to make an impact. I like to think that we did make a big impact. We were part of many people who are doing amazing things to try and convert some of these challenges that neighborhoods and communities like South Side Chicago are facing, but we built a factory and quickly added a hundred jobs, then a hundred more. We're continuing to grow and expand.

Later Whole Foods built a warehouse two doors down. There's now restaurants and all sorts of different commerce coming into play. And if you look statistically, crime rates are down, unemployment is down, violent crime is down. We took the hardest route and did something really big. Scary, at times, how big.

I think it's a great example of not just environmental and social choice but a business choice, because it allowed us to consolidate our supply chain from thousands of miles to tens of miles, so that the footprint of our products on an environmental basis was much, much lower. When you do that, you reduce your costs and become more cost-effective. We had more nimble factories that would be more responsive to customizing our products based on retailer and customer feedback. It was a fully integrated factory. That factory was the answer to so many variables.[11]

Fraser is proving one of the core realities of the Elevated Economy: decisions that provide environmental and social well-being do not necessarily have to be made at the cost of profit. In fact, they can be a major contributing factor to its growth.

---

11 Fraser, discussion with author.

CHAPTER 11

WILLING TO PAY

"True success is overcoming the fear of being unsuccessful."
—Paul Sweeney

S tarbucks earned $26.5 billion in its last fiscal year. But apparently, I'm the only person who contributed to that sum in the Bay Area.

Northern Californians are . . . particular . . . about their coffee. You're more likely to meet a friend at Blue Bottle, Philz, or Verve than you are to spend time with the green-and-white mermaid. When I mention I drink Starbucks to my compatriots, the assumption is that I'm a philistine at best and a tasteless corporate follower at worst. But in reality, my decision to enjoy a Pike Place in the morning is quite carefully calculated. It's a decision I make based on my desire to support the Elevated Economy.

Starbucks is much more than a coffee company. It is a multinational food and beverage conglomerate. Its coffee may not taste quite as incredible as Blue Bottle's, but its ability to influence and improve the lives of people is much greater. When I buy my coffee from Starbucks, I am exercising the same type of choice that every consumer in the Elevated Economy does on a daily basis: I am using my dollars to vote. Not to vote for the company that makes the best coffee, but to vote for the company that makes the best world.

According to the most recent information, Starbucks currently owns and operates 30,626 stores in 76 countries. Those stores are staffed by over 300,000 employees. To put that in perspective, General Mills has 40,000 employees, General Motors has 178,000 employees, and General Electric has 283,000 employees. That means the place you get your morning cup of java has a bigger army than the three biggest generals in Western commerce. But it isn't the size of its workforce that makes me interested in supporting Starbucks; it's the way those workers are treated and the operations they are trained to execute.

Starbucks matches 401(k) payments, even for part-time employees. It also offers every single employee a stock accrual package. The Starbucks Partner Achievement Program offers all full-time and part-time employees free tuition to Arizona State's online university—which was at one time the second-highest-rated online university in the United States and one that consistently fluctuates within the top ten. Finally, all full- and part-time employees at Starbucks are given comprehensive health care as long as they work at least 20 hours a week. In fact, according to *Forbes,* Starbucks spends more on employee benefits than it does on coffee.

All of these benefits and more are outlined in an employee handbook given to every new hire called "Your Special Blend," the opening paragraphs of which highlight just how committed Starbucks is to employee health, satisfaction, and success: "Starbucks simply could not succeed without the passion and determination of our partners. And we believe that success is best when shared."

Most companies preach a similar message in an attempt to motivate and inspire its workers, but Starbucks has become a leader in food and beverage employment by quite literally putting its money where its mouth is. None of the benefits listed previously are cheap, and none of them are easy. But, according to an article in the human resources online news site Snag, all of those payments are paying off.

The article, titled "How Starbucks Conquered Employee Turnover," digs into the company's ability to keep attrition rates so low for so long. According to the article, the average attrition rate for "fast-casual" food and beverage jobs ranges between 150 and 400 percent. McDonald's likes to say it offers the "best first job in America," but that first job quickly leads to a second. Starbucks, on the other hand, has a 65 percent turnover rate for its employees.

According to a recent Gallup Poll, only 32 percent of workers at any job in the United States feel truly engaged by their careers, and workplace apathy is cited as a major contributing factor to employee turnover and corporate churn. Snag estimates that the average rehiring cost for an hourly employee is just over $2,000 each. For firms with staff the size of Starbucks, that could quickly become a multi-million-dollar expense—not to mention costs accrued by other drags on the bottom line that turnover creates. In multiple interviews, former Starbucks executive chairman and CEO Howard Schultz has confirmed again and again how important his employees are to the business that he grew from a handful of roasters in Seattle to one of the most powerful and profitable corporations on the planet.

As his retirement loomed, Schultz was profiled by *Forbes* in an article that posited that the soon-to-depart CEO's most significant impact on the overall business landscape would not be supply chain logistics or real estate management, but would in fact be the way he handled his labor. He is famously quoted as saying:

Our mission statement about treating people with respect and dignity is not just words but a creed we live by every day. You can't expect your employees to exceed the expectations of your customers if you don't exceed the employees' expectations of management.[1]

There's a reason Starbucks refers to its workers as "partners," and that's why I give them my business. I like knowing that the money I spend there is providing not just a job, but a decent job for some of the 300,000 people who work there. I like to think about what businesses those 300,000 people will visit and who else will be supported or encouraged by my purchase. It's important to me that the dollars I spend benefit more than just myself, and that sense of community is at the core of consumer behavior in the Elevated Economy.

When we talk about consumers in business schools, we often use the term "willing to pay" or WTP. It means that there is some combination of the four P's (product, price, place, and promotion) that will get a real person to reach into their wallet and make a purchase. The discussions always center around ways to increase WTP. The fifth "P," as my friend Bianca Gates, CEO of Birdies, mentioned, is Purpose. Consumers need to know that their purchase is supporting a purpose that aligns with their own values and identity. One of the best ways to find new customers is to honestly elevate the way your company operates. There is no way to fake this, and there will be nowhere to hide if you try to.

---

1   https://www.businessinsider.com/howard-schultz-quotes-2012-11.

THE LEADERS

I've had the great pleasure of interviewing many leaders of the new Elevated Economy. These are people who have been consistently producing incredible results by creating products or services that consumers are willing to pay for. The reason they are able to create companies that consumers care about is because they genuinely care themselves. They aren't pretending to care about the environment, their employees, or their vendors; they actually do.

An Elevated Economy is only possible with elevated leaders. All of their businesses have a fifth P, and those purposes are the key to their success.

BLAKE MYCOSKIE—TOMS SHOES

TOMS Shoes founder Blake Mycoskie discovered early on, the power of a business that benefits more than just their customers. From the beginning, their bold strategy of giving away one pair of shoes for every pair they sell was received warmly by millions of consumers. TOMS showed the world that shoes without a designer label or a trendy swoosh can still sell—not because they are better, but because they are accomplishing better things for the world.

The success of TOMS was analyzed and the results compiled into a case study by economic intelligence firm Business Today. One of the most fascinating things about the case is just how much value TOMS was able to get out of one simple, positive decision. Their commitment to doing good allowed them to improve almost every aspect of their business, not just their products.

The good they were able to do became their product, and that product was tailor-made for marketing. Because their purpose-driven message was so strong, TOMS was able to create social media campaigns with simple images of smiling orphans in India. That's a message that no competitor can overcome with a lower price or improved insole. You can't motivate people to act against their own self-interest, and in an Elevated Economy, that self-interest includes the interests of others. TOMS got there early, and both they and those they support have reaped the benefits ever since.

One of the biggest takeaways from the Toms case study is this:

> The power of the social causes and CSR [corporate social responsibility] activities being directly linked to the purchase of company products in the for-profit business. Customers feel they are directly driving higher investment in CSR activities and this is key to the success of this model, and that aspect of it (the direct link from purchase to CSR) could be mirrored in many other business areas.[2]

What was once an outlier is quickly becoming accepted practice; everywhere you look, more and more businesses have stopped shaking their heads at Mycoskie or marveling quietly at the success of his little-business-that-could, and they have started to do what companies do when they smell success: they copy.

TOMS had a fifth P before anyone was really paying attention, and not all companies in the Elevated Economy have such a clear and demonstrable purpose as giving away free pairs of shoes—but that isn't what other firms are copying in the Elevated Economy. What they want now is Mycoskie's ability to quickly connect a consumer with a purpose worth voting for. Whether it's clothing orphans or

---

2   https://www.mckinsey.com/featured-insights/leadership/making-the-most-of-corporate-social-responsibility.

supporting a college student working at Starbucks, consumers expect their companies to give them the ability to support something to care about—not just to give them something to buy.

There have been articles and analyses about TOMS Shoes and the model that Mycoskie popularized in the years since he launched his company. Some argue that providing free shoes robs local markets of the chance to create their own businesses. Some have accused him of being a savior who does more harm than good. It must be noted that TOMS did not immediately identify the unintended consequences of their CSR initiative, but they did adjust the means by which they engaged in philanthropy. As Mike Montgomery wrote in *Forbes*:

> Giving away shoes can hurt local cobblers, which disrupts the local economy. And it risks creating an economy of dependence. While it's much safer for kids to be running around with shoes than without, Toms' charity didn't address the reasons why they were going without shoes in the first place.
>
> Toms (which has expanded into coffee and other products) has since gone back to the drawing board and come up with more thoughtful forms of giving. The company now donates a birth kit (which includes a clean pad, gloves and sterile equipment to cut the baby's umbilical cord) with the sale of every bag. With every bag of coffee the company sells, it gives money to help provide clean water. And while Toms still donates shoes, it now tries to source them from local producers to help strengthen struggling economies.[3]

---

3 https://www.forbes.com/sites/mikemontgomery/2015/04/28/how-entrepreneurs-can-avoid-the-philanthropy-pitfalls/#7536422b1c38.

One thing that firms operating in the Elevated Economy have proven is that establishing a positive purpose can create an almost unbreakable willingness to pay in the consumers it connects with.

CHRISTINA STEMBEL—FARMGIRL FLOWERS

Farmgirl Flowers is a pretty simple company on paper: they deliver flowers. However, founder Christina Stembel has elevated her relatively ordinary business by embracing what I call the five-dollar-tomato principle.

Businesses are complicated but profits are not. Revenue – Expenses = Profit. Simple as that. Businesses are adept at finding ways to make the number to the right of the equals sign as large as possible. This can often lead to some distortions about the real cost of a product or service. You might be able to buy tomatoes at the grocery store for $2 per pound, but that price does not reflect what they should cost. In a world where tomatoes are sourced ethically and grown without pesticides, the actual cost of a tomato should be somewhere closer to $5 a pound. The $2 price reflects cheap immigrant labor, pesticides, genetically modified crops, cost-cutting, early harvesting, and price manipulation. But, at the end of the day, tomatoes should cost around $5 per pound, and when they don't, it should cause us to pause and think, "Why not?"

Stembel has adopted the five-dollar-tomato philosophy in the world of flower delivery. Her bouquets are beautiful, lovingly crafted, and ethically sourced. And what's more, her business actually provides a good quality of life for her workers, and a fair price to the growers, vendors, suppliers, and distributors she works with. I know that every time I buy a bouquet from Farmgirl Flowers, I am supporting one of the most elevated companies in the space. My dollars aren't just getting me flowers, they're helping one business support and sustain many others.

In the company's own words:

> We promise to source our flowers ethically and honestly. We are proud to support farms who pay living wages, avoid harmful chemicals, and have medical benefits for their teams. We strive to partner with as many farms as possible so we can help them create good jobs as well. We are committed to supporting as many American flower farmers as we can, even when it costs more.[4]

The final product may cost a few extra dollars, but those dollars are just more votes that consumers get to cast in favor of a company treating every level of its supply chain ethically. A good tomato should cost more than a couple of bucks. A beautiful bouquet delivered direct to your door should cost more than $25. In the Elevated Economy, business leaders are giving consumers an option to do good, and they are finding a receptive audience.

DREW FRASER—METHOD

Next time you're visiting a friend and need to wash your hands, check the label on their soap. You might see the word METHOD printed neatly on a modern, transparent bottle. Method is winning market share and invading stores around the world by committing to cleaning more than just our bodies.

I first met Drew Fraser, Method's president and CEO, at an event honoring wounded veterans back in 2015. We immediately

---

4 https://farmgirlflowers.com/the-farmgirl-way.

connected and I was genuinely impressed with all the elevated tactics he was employing for a business as simple as soap. Cleaning products were not a category that has to be disrupted with Elevated concepts in order to succeed. People typically just buy whatever brand they have grown up with, or maybe what they have seen next to the faucet of someone they hope to emulate. Method is not "high end" or "designer" soap; you can find it in Target and Walmart at very affordable prices. But Drew is radically committed to making sure that the work his company does creates purpose and provides a narrative of extending benefits beyond the purchases his customers are making.

My personal motto, and one that I believe could lie below the official crest of the Elevated Economy, is to effect positive change at scale. Drew and his company are excellent examples of this in action. He's taken nearly every level of his soap business and spent the time, money, and effort it takes to elevate them and create a new standard for the industry.

In more than one article, Method is cited as "single-handedly turning the packaged goods industry on its head."

Whether it's the products they make or how they make them, the dream of Drew and his former roommate and co-founder Eric Ryan has remained the same: clean the environment while helping people clean themselves. Environmental consumer packaged goods (CPG) watchdog Inhabitat recently did an in-depth analysis of Method's products to determine just how well Eric and Drew are living up to their lofty ideals. This is what they found:

> Every single ingredient in their formulas, including packaging materials, is assessed and scored by the Environmental Protection and Encouragement Agency, an independent research institute led by Dr. Michael Braugart, author of *Cradle*

to Cradle. Method has been recognized by Dr. Braugart and his team as a Cradle to Cradle company, a holistic way of creating products that Method has integrated into every part of the company. Method also works with the Design for the Environment (DfE) office of the US Environmental Protection Agency (EPA), which has recognized more than 50 of their products to be safe for people and the environment.

Their packaging is not only cool, but it also carries a conscience. All of Method's bottles are completely recyclable and made from 100% recycled plastic whenever possible. The design of the packages themselves is scored against Method's very own "green card" program, which ensures that the packaging design considers recyclability, packaging weight, reusability and compostability.

Method's greenness also seeps into company policies, as they are actively making efforts to be a completely carbon-neutral business and have purchased wind and solar energy credits to offset their carbon footprint. Their building is LEED-certified and has recycling and composting systems (with the worms to prove it) set up throughout. They even offer financial incentives to encourage employee use of public or self-propelled transportation to and from the office.

Finally, Method is beginning to look at their supply chain. They have additional financial incentives set in place for suppliers that employ sustainability initiatives including on-site renewable energy generation and the use of energy-efficient equipment. Additionally, they've formed partnerships with the largest contract carrier in the US to ship products in Method-branded trucks that run on biodiesel. With energy- and water-efficiency reporting programs in place at all factories,

Method worked closely with one factory to find a way to recapture all process water, losing none of it down the drain.[5]

Drew doesn't have to do this. Believe it or not, there are currently no federally mandated standards for cosmetic cleaning products outside of a few basic safety regulations outlined by the FDA. The soap they make is not required to be this good for the environment or for their customers. But that's why Method is such a great example of how willingness to pay works in the Elevated Economy.

Purpose propels businesses to start doing what they know they should do. And in the Elevated Economy, purpose is now a prerequisite for connecting to customers and increasing willingness to pay for your products and services.

WHAT ELEVATED LEADERS DO BEST

In this economy, purpose is an oftentimes deciding factor in driving willingness to pay. Specifically, there are three lessons we can learn from the example of companies like TOMS, Method, and Farmgirl Flowers.

NUMBER ONE: SELL TO BELIEVERS

It's vital that businesses in the Elevated Economy abandon the idea of going to market and start adopting strategies that go to *their* markets. Not all markets are created equal and not all consumers will buy what you're selling. This is Business 101, but it's especially important for success as customers continue to evolve. Each of the businesses we highlighted in this chapter are run by leaders who know the value

---

5 https://inhabitat.com/is-it-green-method-home-products/.

of purpose and are capable of communicating that purpose to the consumers who will care most about it. Elevated businesses don't just sell soap, they sell soap that cleans the world, because that's what their true believers—their new customers—are ready to respond to.

NUMBER TWO: DON'T SELL PRODUCTS, TELL STORIES

"Tell, don't sell" is an age-old business trope but, again, it is finding renewed relevance and increased importance as customers shift to valuing *who you are* more than what you sell. Take a look at advertising for the next few days, and you'll find very few direct price points or doorbuster sales called out specifically. What you'll likely see are mini-documentaries that tell stories about how the company aligns with your values, and why you (and your wallet) should support them. If these stories are told honestly and well, they can have the desired effect. A good litmus test for leaders hoping to transition well into the Elevated Economy is to ask the question "What is the story we are telling?" and from there to ask, "How can we tell it even better than we are today?"

NUMBER THREE: DON'T BE AFRAID OF THE FIVE-DOLLAR TOMATO

None of the products or services discussed in this chapter are as cheap as they possibly could be. Every leader has made decisions that intentionally price their products fairly, in the name of creating greater benefit. Whether it's supporting a vendor, an employee, the environment, or all of the above, elevated businesses know that value lives everywhere—not just in the simple formula of revenue minus expenses. Honest and genuine storytelling about who you are can inform and align your customers' willingness to pay.

Business leaders know how much a tomato should cost, but what makes the Elevated Economy so unique and what drives so many of its best leaders is that now customers know it too.

CHAPTER 12

WHOM DO YOU SERVE?

"A mind that is stretched by a new experience can never go back to its old dimensions."
—Oliver Wendell Holmes

One of the biggest problems facing the modern economy is the chasm between what we *should* care about and what we *actually* care about. This is particularly true for businesses. Corporations have always had more power to do good than we gave them credit for, but for generations they were allowed to be distracted by shareholder value while the fires of apathy raged on the other side of the chasm. Above everything else, the Elevated Economy exists because consumers eventually looked over and noticed the flames.

The demands on those in power have changed in a very real way. Fifty years ago, it was enough to provide high-quality products at fair prices, but those days are ending. They may, in fact, already be over. As we've seen earlier in this book, consumers in the new economy care about big issues and, for the first time in history, they are demanding that companies care as well. Consumers have always had more power in the economy than CEOs and analysts give them credit for. But now they are proving it.

By sheer strength of will, consumers have reached across the chasm and begun pulling the two sides together in spectacular fashion. Once they finally meet, the time for "exploratory" conversations will be over. Their union will create a new reality for companies both big and small. As the sides merge, the line between ourselves and our wallets will be inexorably intertwined. In that brave new world, attracting and retaining consumers will no longer be a matter of product, price, place, and promotion. It will become a matter of Purpose.

Back to Birdies CEO Bianca Gates:

> Consumers are now focused on very purpose-driven busi-nesses, so you think about businesses like Everlane or obviously Birdies, there's a lot of new businesses that are cen-tered around giving back to the environment, to people, to economic growth, and more.
>
> People right now are pissed that the planet is on fire, that women are underrepresented, and that minority women in particular are underserved and underrepresented. And so, if we can be louder and prouder about serving those that are being underserved and underrepresented and being a company that's focused on that, I think we will ultimately win by giving back to others and helping them win.[1]

It's fitting, then, for Deloitte to compile a study called "2030 Purpose." In the report, Deloitte's leadership encourages businesses

---

1 Gates, discussion with author.

to map their corporate goals to the "Sustainable Development Goals" established recently by the United Nations.[2] These goals include commitments to clean drinking water around the globe, the eradication of preventable diseases, dramatic reductions in education gaps, and others. Deloitte's 2030 Purpose is a promise that it will join the fight to ". . . provide a comprehensive framework for the world to work together to create a better future to 2030. Businesses can make a huge impact toward the achievement of the Sustainable Development Goals and the good news is that this isn't just good for humanity, it's good for business."[3]

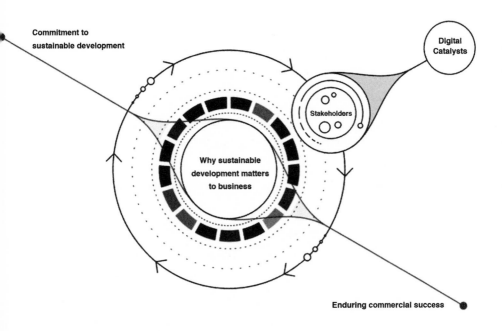

In his opening remarks, Deloitte executive David Cruickshank highlights the synergy between value, values, sustainability, and profit. He writes:

> The route to unlocking the benefits of 2030 Purpose will differ by business and sector. However, there are some golden rules: authenticity, balance and consistent application.
>
> An authentic purpose is one that is lived through the actions of the business. A balance needs to be continually maintained between emphasis on short-term imperatives and longer-term external commitments, whilst understanding developing stakeholder expectations. Finally, the purpose should be applied consistently, enduring well into the future and transcending corporate changes. 2030 Purpose is a choice, and a choice that has many implications. But it is a choice that is increasingly recognized as a necessary condition for the delivery of long-term value, both to direct stakeholders and wider society.
>
> It's good for business and good for the world.[4]

According to Deloitte, the key to "connecting sustainable development with enduring commercial success" is a commitment to "sustainable development."

This development, as the study outlines, will be achieved as Deloitte shifts its corporate values to precisely mirror the UN's Sustainable Development Goals (SDGs). This is a historic moment for the way businesses operate.

Deloitte is not a small company or part of a niche, cottage industry. It is one of the "Big Four" accounting and consultancy firms and generates over $40 billion in revenue each year. Its decision to align

4 Ibid.

its values to mirror the UN's SDGs is not mere lip service. Deloitte has made its new system public, and fully incorporates the UN's standards as its own. Deloitte is actually evolving from a shareholder-value-focused company to a purpose-driven organization. And its CEO, Punit Renjen, is happy to explain why. He writes in the report, "Purpose answers the critical questions of who a business is and why it exists beyond making a profit, through a set of carefully articulated core beliefs. But, to be more than just words, purpose must guide behavior, influence strategy, transcend leaders—and endure."[5]

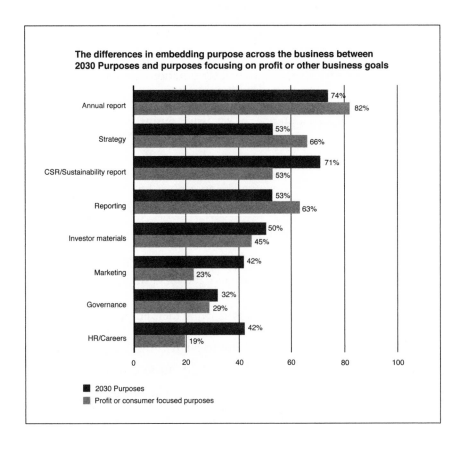

The differences in embedding purpose across the business between 2030 Purposes and purposes focusing on profit or other business goals

Annual report: 74% / 82%
Strategy: 53% / 66%
CSR/Sustainability report: 71% / 53%
Reporting: 53% / 63%
Investor materials: 50% / 45%
Marketing: 42% / 23%
Governance: 32% / 29%
HR/Careers: 42% / 19%

■ 2030 Purposes
▨ Profit or consumer focused purposes

---

5 https://www2.deloitte.com/us/en/pages/about-deloitte/articles/culture-of-purpose.html.

The last revolution to drive a change this fundamental was the Internet. The web connected people to firms commercially. At the time, the thinking was that this would make consumers more accessible and malleable to the whims of Wall Street. But the effect has proven to be the reverse. Instead of corporations more heavily influencing customers, customers are more heavily influencing corporations.

Consumers are driving changes in large-scale social, environmental, and humanitarian progress by the ways they choose to spend their dollars. Businesses the size of Deloitte, Amazon, and others have already realized this and have rushed to adapt. But they might still be too slow. According to Deloitte's 2030 Purpose:

> Discussions with large and small organizations, public and private, combined with research on the top 150 of the FTSE350 have highlighted a number of key issues businesses face in trying to achieve 2030 Purpose.
>
> While two thirds of large businesses have a purpose of some description, only a quarter make an explicit link with a wider social, environmental or economic goal. Of those companies which link the purpose with sustainable development, half explicitly embed the purpose in strategy. The imperative for purpose is there and executives recognize that there is a need.

So why aren't more businesses living their purpose?[6]

Deloitte and others who choose to align with objective, progressive business goals like the UN's and 2030 Purpose aren't just adding a few more line items on their annual report. They are actively recreating their corporate priorities from the ground up.

---

6   Ibid.

Not all priorities are equal. Some, such as culture, brand, and reporting, are more difficult to bring into the fold than facilities or internal communications. But the time to act has come, and leaders at firms like Deloitte know it. They know that if action isn't taken and sustainability isn't prioritized through purpose, then the future we are marching toward won't have the capacity to keep pace with businesses the way they used to. In his closing statement, Renjen makes a bold statement:

. . . In the near term, if businesses don't align around 2030 Purpose, skepticism towards sustainable development may become legitimate just as stakeholders lose faith in the contribution business can make.

In the medium and longer term, without the dedicated effort of the business factor, social and environmental progress will stall. Opportunities to promote inclusion, equality and stability will diminish. Carbon emissions and natural disasters will continue to rise. Without the positive power of business, our people and planet will decay. For business, the impacts of technological change are likely to cause ever deepening challenges.

Today, digital technology disrupts every industry. Tomorrow, we can expect this to accelerate as exponential technologies take hold. Many authors predict that as artificial intelligence gets smarter, more humans will be pushed out of the job market as businesses ultimately become led by algorithms rather than people. In this climate, there is a growing need for businesses to establish themselves as forces for good, worth protecting for our collective future.[7]

---

7 Ibid.

Renjen—and leaders like him—realize that you can't make a profit off a dying planet. He realizes that inclusion leads to greater profit than exclusion. And for businesses to progress, so must humanity in general. Because, as a recent *Forbes* article titled "Why purpose needs to be a pivotal part of your business strategy" states:

> The secret to better and bigger work may not be better and bigger numbers. A recent study from Korn Ferry showed that companies with teams focused on their organization's purpose had annual growth rates nearly three times the annual rate for their entire industry.
>
> According to the survey, 90 percent of people who worked in a purpose-driven organization reported feeling engaged in their work. In companies that aren't as focused on purpose, only 32 percent of employees reported feelings of engagement and connectedness with the work they were doing.[8]

The path to these profits takes time, commitment, and resources. But like all great journeys, it begins with a single step. Or, in this case, a single question.

WHOM DO WE SERVE?

The answer to this question, for the last 50 years, has been straightforward. Fifty years ago, the economist Milton Friedman advanced the theory of Shareholder Primacy, stating that "corporations have no higher purpose than maximizing profits for their shareholders," and

---

8   https://www.forbes.com/sites/williamvanderbloemen/2017/01/29/why-purpose-should-be-a-pivotal-part-of-your-business-strategy/#4a19f4084135.

therefore, shareholder interests should be placed ahead of all other stakeholders.

This list of needs typically began and ended with shareholder value. But, in the world after the Business Roundtable's groundbreaking proclamation that shareholder value should no longer be king, and as we move closer to the full impact of the Great Wealth Migration and all the implications and power shifts that come with it, we begin to see a radically different—and still highly profitable—playbook being written and standardized.

This playbook provides a very different answer to the question of whom your business can, and should, serve while still turning a profit. Today, as business leaders plan and strategize, they may very well be transitioning from "we exist to serve the needs of the business" to "our business exists to serve the needs of the world." In doing so, they have sparked, and will eventually sustain and ratify, the largest shift in capitalist doctrine in history. The potential implications should be as inspiring to the soul as they are to the corporate balance sheet.

Just a few years ago, this was a mere theory, one that author Aaron Hurst theorized about in his book *The Purpose Economy*. According to Hurst, back in the halcyon days of 2014:

> In the last ten years, social innovation has become big business. Conferences and magazines are dedicated to the topic, and legions of consultants and entrepreneurs help individuals and companies adapt to this new way of operating. Under President Obama, the White House now has an Office of Social Innovation and Civic Participation.
>
> . . . Much like technology a few decades ago, purpose has now become a business imperative. In today's world, running an organization without an intentional emphasis on purpose

for employees and customers is like running an organization in the early 1990s and failing to implement technology.

. . . At its foundation, the Purpose Economy creates purpose for people. It serves the critical need for people to develop themselves, be part of a community, and affect something greater than themselves. It may sound utopian, but there is evidence in almost every industry and throughout our culture that this shift is already underway. The Information Economy, which has driven innovation and economic growth for approximately the past fifty years, is only the most recent evolutionary leap in the history of the global economy. We are now in the process of making the next big leap.[9]

We are no longer in the process of making this leap. We are now at the height of its bell curve. The past decade has made the potential for profitable purpose-driven companies possible, but the decade to come is when we will begin our descent. By its end, the corporate world will have fully stuck a brand-new landing in brand-new territory. A territory where "whom we serve" and "how we perform" will have become welded into a single, inseparable concept. In that world, creating shareholder value will occur, but it will occur as a result of creating real environmental, social, and human value, rather than being at their expense.

According to the World Economic Forum, the future of business is "Purpose, Not Just Profit." Of course, you still need to turn a profit. Of course, quality, affordability, and logistics all still matter. But in the Elevated Economy—in the new world order of ESG, socially

---

9 *The Purpose Economy: How Your Desire for Impact, Personal Growth and Community Is Changing the World* (Elevate, 2016), 3.

responsible investing, conscious capitalism, and dramatic changes in what consumers are willing to vote for with their dollars—those things will become by-products of purpose, and not the other way around. The Forum made this clear in no uncertain terms:

> In business, CEOs have gone from being symbols of aspiration to objects of intense scrutiny. Even the younger, "cooler" entrepreneurs, the kick-starters of the shared economy, are now being asked questions about the impact their companies have on society. Trust has become the ultimate currency.
>
> Millennial consumers are driving this trend; 40% of those polled by the Deloitte Millennial Survey 2018 believe the goal of businesses should be to "improve society." This is seriously worth pondering. By 2020, Millennials will make up 40% of all consumers, influencing about $40 billion in annual sales.
>
> Profit with purpose is set to become the new norm. Up to this point, social enterprise and impact investment have been driving this concept, which has somehow remained confined to a niche. Not anymore. Now, it's all set to change: the CEOs of the future will want their companies to be recognized as forces for good.[10]

We are currently at the beginning of a world-changing economic shift. The tipping point is only starting to be reached. But when the tip happens, it will happen fast, and only those firms that made intentional decisions to establish more clever footing will remain standing. And, in many ways, all roads lead back to ESG.

---

10 https://www.weforum.org/agenda/2019/01/why-businesses-must-be-driven-by-purpose-as-well-as-profits/.

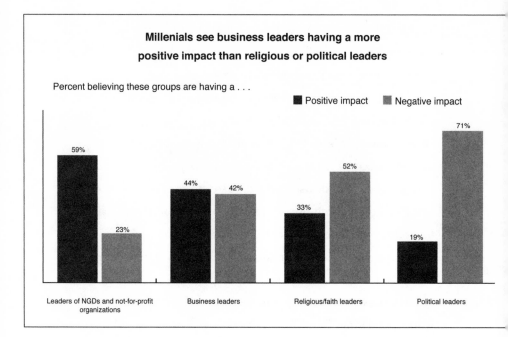

**Millenials see business leaders having a more
positive impact than religious or political leaders**

Percent believing these groups are having a . . .

■ Positive impact   ■ Negative impact

| Leaders of NGDs and not-for-profit organizations | Business leaders | Religious/faith leaders | Political leaders |
| 59% / 23% | 44% / 42% | 33% / 52% | 19% / 71% |

In its concluding remarks, the report from the World Economic Forum says:

> With the growing trend for investors and consumers to buy into companies that deliver positive social change alongside financial returns, the trend for big business to adopt impactful social missions looks set to continue. The question is: how many business leaders will have the courage to step up to the plate? The business of changing the world is in their hands.[11]

Those hands are yours. That time is now. The question is begging to be answered. Whom are you going to serve?

---

11   Ibid.

ALL WHO COME

"To all who come to this happy place, welcome."

Those were the words spoken by Walt Disney when he opened Disneyland to the public for the very first time in July of 1955.

Today, beloved business leaders like Walt might seem few and far between. Disney was far from perfect, but none of us are. Whether you run a massive hedge fund, serve in the C-suite, or work in middle management, it's never been more important to appreciate the value of every decision you make and every goal you set. The human race is finally entering a phase where companies really can "do well by doing good," and—call me an optimist—I believe this phase will be the richest in human history.

In every sense of the word.

The choice is no longer between profits or purpose. The two are now inextricably linked and their order has been miraculously reversed. Consumer behavior will continue to drive and shape the economy in the decades to come. But the shape those consumers are making is as beautiful as it is unrecognizable to the economic thinking of yesterday.

The "founding fathers" of this revolution on the corporate side are the members of the Business Roundtable who penned a new Declaration of Independence on August 9, 2019, when they officially moved stakeholder above shareholder. Keeping a historical perspective, we are now in the first Constitutional Convention. It is the job of every business leader today to take their seat at the table and align with consumers who are demanding a better world for themselves today and for their children tomorrow. Or, as the Roundtable itself puts it:

> Business Roundtable CEOs believe we have a responsibility
> to help build a strong and sustainable economic future in the

United States. That means creating quality jobs and good wages and benefits. It requires action to increase opportunity and raise living standards. It demands advancing public policies that better enable people of all backgrounds to achieve their potential. Together with partners in the public, private and non-profit sectors, Business Roundtable CEOs are committed to driving solutions that make a meaningful difference for workers, families, communities and businesses of all sizes.

. . . These investments and initiatives aren't just about doing good; they're about doing good business and creating a thriving economy with greater opportunity for all.[12]

There has never been a more exciting time to lead or influence a business. There has never been more potential for positivity and progress in capitalism. The decisions we make now can create a new and brighter economic landscape, one where your soul, and the planet, can remain intact without sacrificing the success of your enterprise. As business leaders, the new economy, and all the opportunities it affords, has brought each of us to the most significant inflection point of our careers.

Don't miss it.

The economy has elevated itself to a higher standard. It's time for us to do the same.

---

12 https://www.businessroundtable.org.

CONCLUSION

You've heard it a thousand times: innovate or die.

Consumers and investors have elevated their game. They have innovated. And now, you have to innovate with them. Or face the consequences.

I tried to lean in to the "the end is near" rhetoric as much as possible in this book. Not because I enjoy being dramatic, but because I believe that the tsunami is coming. That the tides have receded. That the wave is on the way. That it's very nearly here.

I don't have a time machine, but when it comes to economics, a bit of research and the wisdom of some very intelligent people can be just as good for dodging calamity.

It is also important to drive home the optimistic side of the Elevated Economy. Profit margins and revenue predictions aside, we are approaching a truly thrilling age for businesses and those who lead them. We no longer have to lead our companies at society's expense. Whether it's providing safer, healthier working conditions, or making decisions that are in the best interest of the environment, the choice between doing well or doing good no longer has to be made.

The Elevated Economy is here. You now know how your next customers' and investors' thinking has changed. You know how they evaluate your company before making a purchase decision, and how they vote with their dollars. You know how to begin an authentic plan for change, and how to compete by telling who you are, not selling what you make.

This is the sort of world I dreamed about before I moved to New York City to start my first business. I saw New York as a land of possibility—a place where dreams happen while you're awake—and I wanted to be a part of it. I feel the exact same way about the next few decades of economic progress. What happens next doesn't just have to be great. It can also be good.

Pundits and analysts are always saying how "this is going to change everything"—and I suppose that now I must include myself in that list.

But I truly believe it. I believe that consumers are the kings of capitalism. As they go, so, too, do we—and they are on the move in much larger numbers, and at a much more aggressive pace, than we have seen in a long time. At the end of their journey is an economic landscape where the businesses that perform best can also be the businesses that do the best. And for me, nothing could be more inspiring or exciting.

What about you?

ACKNOWLEDGMENTS

This book would not have been possible without the help and support of so many. I want to say thank you to my wife, whose support has been unwavering since day one.

Thank you to my parents. Mom, you're the smartest PhD, and the most dedicated mom anyone could ever have. And Dad, you're the definition of the phrase "actions speaking louder than words." I hope I can be as good a moral compass for my children as you have been to me.

To my children—I love you immeasurably. You have taught me more than you could possibly imagine. I'm looking forward to the next steps of our adventure together.

Ted, I could never have done any of this without you. Thank you for your guidance, humor, and friendship since the beginning.

Phil, I hope that one day I am able to repay the debt of gratitude that I owe to you. Thank you.

I definitely owe a debt of gratitude to Harvard Business School for the lifelong friends I met there, for challenging me to go far, far outside my comfort zone, and for all of my incredible professors—I had life-altering experiences because of you.

Thanks to the people at Fast Company for believing that these ideas are worth spreading.

Thanks to you, dear reader. This is an exciting and positive time for business and humanity in general. We finally have an economic model for a future we can believe in. One that exists for the good of everyone.

Let's enjoy it together.

INDEX

NUMBERS

ABOUT THE AUTHOR

Richard Steel is an American entrepreneur, investor, and consultant. He has run private and public companies, served on nonprofit boards, and advised the White House Business Council. He is an advisor to large and mid-size companies, governments, startups, and nonprofits. Currently, he is the CEO of a venture firm and chairs a philanthropic fund. Richard is an alumnus of Harvard Business School where he serves on the Alumni Board.